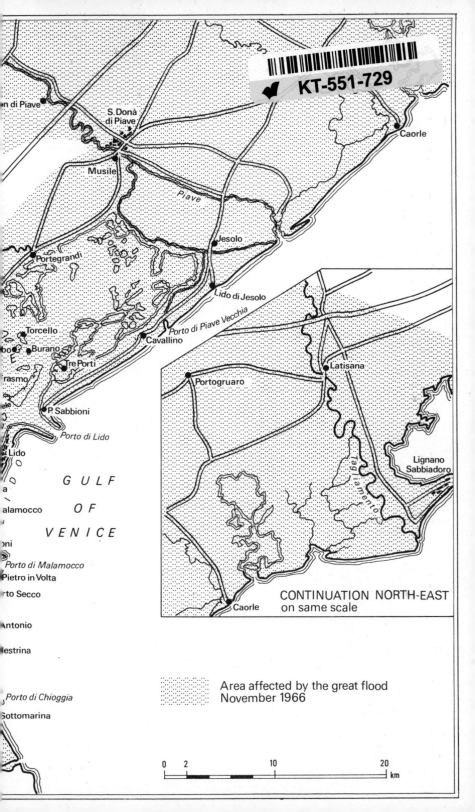

n di Piave

S. Donà
di Piave

Caorle

Musile

Piave

Jesolo

Portegrandi

Lido di Jesolo

Torcello

Porto di Piave Vecchia

Burano

Cavallino

Tre Porti

rasmo

Latisana

P. Sabbioni

Portogruaro

Porto di Lido

Lido

Lignano
Sabbiadoro

GULF

a

alamocco

O F

VENICE

oni

Porto di Malamocco

Pietro in Volta

Tagliamento

to Secco

Antonio

CONTINUATION NORTH-EAST
on same scale

estrina

Caorle

Porto di Chioggia

Sottomarina

Area affected by the great flood
November 1966

0   2   10   20
|___|___|___|___|___|___|___|___|___| km

A World by Itself

SHIRLEY GUITON

A World by Itself

Tradition and change
in the Venetian Lagoon

Illustrations by John Lawrence

Hamish Hamilton · London

First published in Great Britain 1977
by Hamish Hamilton Ltd
90 Great Russell Street, London WC1B 3PT

Copyright © 1977 by Shirley Guiton

SBN 241 89434 4

Typeset by Burns & Harris Ltd, Dundee
Printed in Great Britain by
T. & A. Constable Ltd, Edinburgh

For my mother

A world by itself, and we will nothing pay
For wearing our own noses.

Cymbeline

Contents

Preface

This book belongs to the friends who helped me write it:

To my friends in the lagoon who gave me their confidence and whose opinions and way of life I have tried to set down fairly and without distortion. They will not be pleased with everything that I have said but I know they will respect my views as I do theirs;

To Angelo Procaccini who knows more about the lagoon than one would have thought possible in one man;

To official friends, who must be nameless, who use traditional methods and modern techniques to continue to protect the fabric of Venice and the islands of the lagoon;

And to two non-lagoon friends: Ruth Zuntz who with a generous heart provided support and help of many kinds, a welcoming house and the society of five little dogs, and Antonia von Gebsattel who contributed affectionate mockery which writers need and seldom get, and both a constant flow of music;

To all: thank you.

Cà' S. Tomà, Torcello, 1974
Asolo, 1975

1 A Lagoon for Living

The Venetian lagoon is a tribute to man's ingenuity and tenacity. Man first took to this large area of river deltas, marshes, accumulations of river silt, sandbars, all subject to the action of currents, tides and winds, as a place to fish and hunt for food, then as a refuge from danger on the mainland. Once he was permanently settled he began the long process of dominating his environment and changing it to suit his safety, both from the elements and his human enemies, his interests and his industries. It is an activity which continues to this day.

The lagoon which man inherited is made chiefly of sand and silt played on by the action of water and winds. The silt was brought down by the rivers, of which the Brenta, Sile and Piave were the most important, which reached the sea through deltas in the lagoon. In times of great storms in the mountains behind Venice these rivers are still a danger and when in spate must have caused dramatic changes in the lagoon. At the same time seawater attacked the sand dunes protecting the lagoon, and the tides, sometimes

1

spectacularly high tides with the wind behind them, ate away what appeared to be solid land. Normally lagoons succumb to these conditions and gradually silt up. Ravenna is a case in point. It was originally a lagoon city, indeed this was part of its defences against its enemies. Now it lies several miles from the sea in the middle of an undistinguished plain.

Another phenomenon of natural change has been the sinking of the floor of the lagoon. This has been calculated at two millimetres a year in the Quaternary period and perhaps one and a half millimetres a year in early historic times measured by the effect on archaeological remains. In the last forty years or so this rate has increased to about three millimetres a year. This leads to the reasonable assumption that the sinking in prehistoric and early historic times was compensated by the deposit of silt from the rivers which ran through it.

There are other complicating factors. The waters of the lagoon divide into three basins. There are three main entrances to the lagoon, and the tides which pour in through them at different speeds and appear from the surface to be behaving in exactly the same way, are actually three different areas each obeying its own rules without much mixture between one water mass and another. Also the water in the lagoon tends to be higher during daylight in the summer. It decreases in height during the evening and is quite low at night. In the winter the reverse is the case.

Over historic times the lagoon has altered in shape and extent but not to an unrecognisable degree. It extends from the Brenta to the Sile, a distance of some 55 kilometres, and its breadth from the sea to the *terraferma* or mainland varies from about 8 to 15 kilometres. Its area is approximately 550 square kilometres of which nearly 26 square kilometres are land, 430 are water and 92 *barene*, sedgy wastes which are normally only covered by the *acqua alta* or abnormally high tides, and which extend into the *velme* or adjacent areas submerged even by normal tides. On the *barene* and *velme* flourish a multitude of plants (including stretches of sea lavender in the late summer) and birds, though the shyer ones are retreating from the racket of motor-boats into remoter places.

Man started using the lagoon as a place to fish and hunt. Remains have been found of what were probably temporary shelters built by fishermen for themselves and their equipment. Certainly by Roman times fishing was an important industry which was much increased by the early Venetians who preserved and raised fish in vast enclosures, which came to be called *valli*, in the more protected parts of the lagoon. The *casone* of the fishermen also provided shelter for the game birds (mostly mallard and *folaghe*) attracted into the *valli* by the concentration of fish. Consequently sport and the *valli* became linked from an early period.

The first permanent settlements must have dated from about the same period. The Roman Empire had lost both the power and the will to see to the safety of its peripheral provinces. The first settlements in the northern lagoon in Torcello, and the other islands which have now disappeared, seem to have been of refugees from Altino, the Roman city established on the edge of the lagoon. These settlements gave way, in influence and accessibility, to the little city which grew up on the Rialto and which eventually became Venice. It owed its early position of leadership to the fact that it commanded the principal entrance to the lagoon. As the Rialto settlement grew it had two main considerations in mind. The first was to ensure its own safety and the second to encourage the commerce on which it lived. In both cases it turned to the lagoon and combined its two interests in the campaign which ended with the defeat of Pepin, the son of Charlemagne, in 809. He had captured the city of Malamocco which, until then, had been the seat of the Doge. Pepin's force was cut to pieces when the tide left its boats stranded in the tortuous channels of the lagoon. The Republic of Venice paid heed to the lesson and soon after the Doge transferred the seat of his government to the much more secure group of islands where Venice now stands and which were well protected by the intricacies of the waterways and tides. This victory led to gradual independence from Byzantium, while laying the beginnings of commercial enterprise on a wide scale, and to eventual domination in trade with the East. There had, even before that time, been regular lines for the transport of passengers

3

and goods about the lagoon and linking Venice to the neighbouring cities through Fusina, which remained the principal land approach until the railway was built in the nineteenth century. So for convenience of commerce Venice was linked to centres such as Lyons and Milan. Great machines, known as *carri,* hoisted boats over the bank which separated the lagoon from the river Brenta at Fusina.

With increasing wealth and power the Serene Republic began the great engineering works designed to tame the lagoon. First the rivers were, one by one, diverted. This diminished the havoc caused by flooding. The greatest problem was the Piave because of the volume of its waters and the violence of its floods which poured down almost directly from the Alpine foothills some sixty miles away. Originally the Piave had run into the sea near Torcello through a seven-pronged delta. In the fifth century a terrible flood overwhelmed the area and entirely changed the bed of the Piave, discharging it into the sea at Jesolo or Old Piave. Danger of flooding continued and in 1534 the Argine S. Marco (St. Mark's Embankment) was built; it still contains the river in the neighbourhood of S. Donà di Piave. In 1552 a decree describing the Piave as 'the principal enemy of the lagoon' ordered the building of a new outlet near Cortelazzo, on the eastern side of the modern resort of Jesolo. This work was finished in 1683. The second problem was the Brenta. The first cut controlling the waters was made by Padua in 1140 but this gave no satisfaction to the Venice city fathers since its object was land drainage. If anything, it damaged the lagoon by bringing down more silt. In 1300 the Brenta ran into the sea through the Malamocco entrance and later through Fusina. In 1488 it was diverted into the Brentone cut with its outlet at Brondolo, and in 1610 the Taglio Novissimo (newest cut) was finished. It still flows in these channels. Work on the Sile came a little later and lasted for some ten years from 1673. Besides these very sizeable rivers many small streams which ran into the lagoon were also diverted.

These huge and enormously costly works regulated the mass of sweet water running through the lagoon. Precautions were taken against attack from the sea from a very early date. Vestiges of defences dating from the sixth century

4

have been discovered, consisting of wooden stakes driven into the subsoil with a basket wickerwork of thinner branches weaving them together. Sea defence had been regarded as so important to the city that a special magistrate was charged with co-ordinating its safety precautions as well as its adornment. This office was created in 814 when the seat of the Doge was transferred to the islands which now constitute the city. From this early magistrature sprang the Magistratura alle Acque which still has total oversight and control of the lagoon and its defences and which sits majestically in its palace at the foot of the Rialto bridge. The early defences against the sea consisted of earth banks planted with tamarisk and strengthened with coarse gravel rammed behind the stakes which had been driven into the lagoon bed. This type of protection can still be seen in some of the remoter islands. These banks were, however, not suitable protection against the sea as they were soon undermined by the action of the waves. This was dramatically demonstrated during the disastrous storms of 1543, 1686 and 1691 which broke through the defences at Malamocco, Pellestrina and Caroman, which lies on the narrowest strip of land which separates the sea from the lagoon. These were the points of greatest danger and in the eighteenth century the Venetian Republic undertook the tremendous task of building the first of the Murazzi. The order was for the construction of walls 'more durable than bronze'. Work began at Caroman, Malamocco and S. Pietro in Volta. They were designed by a monk, Vincenzio Coronelli, and an architect named Zendrini. The system they devised is still the basic method used in the construction of the sea defences of the lagoon.

Over the centuries the main navigation channels were dredged, deepened, widened and maintained in a state to carry the increasing weight of freight on which the Republic's commerce depended. They were also marked by those groups of stakes so characteristic of the lagoon. They are known collectively as *bricoli*, but if you talk to a fisherman you will find that he refers very precisely to each by its own name. A single stake, though in appearance it is more a tree-trunk than a stake, is called a *mede*, a group of several a

5

bricole, and the *dame* is a *bricole* with the middle stake rising well above the others indicating the entrance to a canal.

One effect of all this work was to increase the population of the lagoon. From a very early period, convents and monasteries whose main houses were in Venice had annexes in various lagoon islands. There were also a number of independent foundations situated in the lagoon. At one time there were said to be a hundred churches in Torcello. This should probably be interpreted as a reference not to the island proper but to the parish which, until quite recent times, covered an extensive area of the northern lagoon and its fringe. The history of many of these foundations shows that life was not always comfortable or easy in the lagoon in spite of the improvements and flood controls which had been contrived. Many of these convents have disappeared altogether with the islands on which they were situated, leaving sometimes only the name of a canal behind them, such as the Benedictine convents cf S. Felice, or S. Lorenzo which was established in the drowned island of Ammiana beyond Torcello. Other houses had to be transferred because living conditions were so difficult. The nuns of Santa Ariana left their convent because it was so inaccessible and, in any case, infested by rats and snakes. Santa Ariana is the rather gruesome island where the Republic deposited the bones of its deceased citizens at the end of their fifteen-year tenure of the graves in the cemetery of S. Michele. It is now a melancholy island, no more than a little ghostly and totally abandoned. The Republic, however, did not choose to have the island abandoned and forced the nuns to return, though eventually it had to concede that the rats and snakes were indeed making life intolerable and rescinded its decision.

But life was not always harsh, nor, indeed, the religious rule strictly adhered to. In the sixteenth century the religious orders in Venice, as elsewhere, went through a period of moral laxness, not to say turpitude. We hear tales of nuns running away with scions of famous patrician houses and a patriarchal decree of May 29, 1509, exhorted abbesses to prevent nuns from strolling about the Piazza in what one might call civvies. They were accused of celebrating Easter as though it were the Carnival and, in particular, that they had danced till dawn with young patricians to the sound of fifes and trumpets.

Other islands were used, as they still are, as isolation hospitals and places where the insane and sick could be cared for. There is, beyond Torcello, a desolate island called La Cura where the ladies of the town were sent to be cured before reinstatement on the list of courtesans. Venice had a careful government, perspicacious, efficient and wise, which lost sight of no single little thing for the protection of the citizenry and particularly of any kind of remunerative tourist activity.

Many islands belonged to the patricians, who used them, as they still do, as summer residences or as shooting lodges. From the earliest times duck shooting has been eagerly followed as a sport and the mallard which come in from the sea to feed in the lagoon are much appreciated as table birds. They were so highly regarded as to constitute a suitable gift from the Doge to the heads of patrician families at Christmas, and a part of the lagoon beyond Torcello is still known as the *Valle* Dogà. As the patrician class grew, the annual present of five ducks to each head of family became a serious burden on the Doge's purse. The Serenissima therefore agreed to the striking of a medal each year to replace the five ducks and they became known as *oselle* or birds. The patrician, even when on pleasure bent, retained a regard for profit, and property in the lagoon was usually organised to include a *valle* or fish farm. They still exist, though not quite so numerous in the northern lagoon as they were. They are normally stocked by lagoon fishermen who go out to catch *novelami* or tiny fish as thin and elusive as a pin. They are let loose in the *valli* and when they have grown big enough are caught in nets and sent to market.

It is paradoxical that the activities which led to such an increase in the population of the lagoon should also have caused its depopulation. The rate of flow of the lagoon waters was slowed down when regulated by the diversion of the rivers. This seems to have led to a higher rate of silting up and the more sluggish waters provided breeding places for mosquitoes and thus malaria. The lagoon which had earlier been subject to swift changes, with islands appearing and dis-

7

appearing, now became stagnant, even fetid in places, and a population threatened by *la febbre* as well as isolation and unemployment tended to drift away. The people of Burano, which has been one of the few continuously inhabited islands, attribute their healthiness to the fact that it is surrounded by deep channels of swiftly moving tidal waters.

With the decay of the power of Venice inertia seeped into nearly all its activities. The embankments defending the lagoon from the encroachment of the sea were neglected and it was the Austrians who rebuilt the Murazzi after Napoleon had handed the defunct Republic and its lands over to the Austro-Hungarian Empire. Similarly the river embankments had been allowed to decay. A breakthrough in the lagoon was much more devastating than on the mainland though that was sufficiently terrifying. This is how Horatio Brown describes one flood:

> During heavy floods the dykes are patrolled day and night by relays of watchmen, who build for themselves rude shelter huts of matting and a little straw. These watchmen camp together in threes, and relieve one another in turns. Each has a lantern, which he fastens to an iron rod, and plants outside the hut, so that at night the river bank is dotted with these little groups of three flames swaying in the breeze. The greatest difficulty and danger in guarding the bank is that all the mischief is done out of sight. The river, sweeping along, loosens a tiny piece of earth far down below the level of its surface. The water continues to bore at this hole, working deeper into the bank, until this is undermined. But the first notice that the watchers receive will be the subsidence of the whole upper mass of earth. Then in a few minutes the waters burst through, flowing far and wide over the vineyards and maize-fields, and making the breach broader every moment. Nothing can be done till the floods go down; and then it is the work of many months to repair even one breach. There is only one way of saving the bank supposing the watchmen to have discovered the mischief in time. The poplars and mulberry trees which grow in abundance in the meadows must be cut and carried to the top of the bank, and there

8

laid in lines along the mound; deep notches are then made in their trunks, and, where the bank shows signs of weakness, a rope is tied to the tree and firmly pegged down, the boughs are weighted with stones, and the whole mass is thrown into the water at the point of danger, forming a dam which thrusts the current into the middle of the river again. It is an expensive remedy, but the only one which stands between the rich meadows and destruction.

The process of decay seems, if anything, to have been hastened on the unification of Italy. Not only had the old energy of the Venetians been sapped through the centuries, but political power and decision-making had been transferred from the old city states to the national capital in Rome. It was pride of independence which had created Venice and enabled it to make the lagoon a defence and a living space for men. Now it was merged in a larger ideal and the change, in some ways, carried a high price. So gradually came the decay that such nineteenth-century writers as Ruskin and Horatio Brown lament.

With industrialisation (sorely needed to provide a reasonable economic basis for Venice and the mainland) came other factors of decay, which, being then unrecognised as the sinister enemies that they are, were not checked at an early stage. These enemies include the pollution of the air and the consequent damage to the stone of which Venice is built, pollution of the water by insoluble chemical effluents, the more rapid subsidence of the lagoon bed as water for industrial purposes was pumped out of the natural reservoir which lies below the lagoon.

There had been warnings of danger. On April 16, 1936, there was a very serious flood which reached 1.47 metres. On November 12, 1951, flood waters reached the height of 1.51 metres. Both floods did enormous damage. The slow sapping of the defences on which Venice's survival depends was, of course, known to the engineers of the Magistratura alle Acque and the Genio Civile who were actually responsible for the work of maintenance and renovation. But there was no money, no foresight on the part of Parliament, which preferred arcane political games to the dull, solid stuff of governing.

The shock of the flood of November 4, 1966, was all the greater. For the first time the Venetians really believed that their city might disappear. For the first time they noticed that the statuary adorning their churches and palaces was flaking off, that at very low water the buildings seemed supported only on the most fragile, encrusted wooden piles, that quays were crooked and bridges leant askew. Even then it required years of negotiation before the Special Law of Venice was passed through Parliament.

It would, however, be wrong to think that nothing was done during these years. National and municipal money was made available, not always soon enough and not always enough at a time, to allow for essential work. Since 1966 ten billion lire have been spent.

The first and most urgent work was to repair and generally strenghten the Murazzi which run from the Chioggia to the Malamocco entrance to the lagoon. At Caroman at the Chioggia end of the lagoon, the strip of land is scarcely wider than the sea defences. At Pellestrina and S. Pietro in Volta the land is just wide enough to accommodate a few little fields, protected by hedges and reed fences, between the sea wall and the tall houses of the village. The old houses have few, if any, windows facing the sea and this gives a bleak, almost prison-like appearance to the villages, which is belied by the gaiety and warmth of the façade facing the lagoon. There can be no doubt that the sea is regarded as an enemy.

The system adopted in rebuilding the Murazzi and the great containing embankments is the traditional one first used in the seventeenth century. The techniques used are modern. The first line of defence is made of huge blocks of rough cut stone or ferro-concrete tetrapodes dropped into the sea to make a great barrier whose purpose is to break the force of the waves before they reach the embankment. Then there is a strip of beach and then the embankment proper, nowadays faced with stone or sometimes concrete. The original defence works are hidden somewhere in the heart of this embankment. Along the top there is a wall of squared-off blocks of masonry. On the landward side is a wide concrete path along which one can walk almost the whole way from Caroman to S. Pietro in Volta. Then the earth embankment, which on this side is normally held together with grass or small bushes, slopes down to the main road running along the coast.

Within the lagoon an enormous programme of work has been carried out, though, as the engineers themselves are the first to say, there is still a great deal to be done. There are several systems for protecting island coasts, the banks of canals in the city and in the islands, but they are all variations of driven piles of wood or ferro-concrete called *palancole,* some masculine and some feminine, dovetailing into a strong fence. Behind these there is a line of ferro-concrete *pali* (stakes) and the space between them is filled with rammed pebbles. The *palancole* and *pali* and the pebbled filling are driven into the bed of the lagoon below the surface of the water. On top of them is built a stout ferro-concrete platform which carries the visible part of the embankment. This is usually made of dressed stone, backed by a stout ferro-concrete wall.

Whenever possible traditional methods have been used. As in the case of Agostino Amadi's boat-building business, modern tools and equipment make the work easier and more precise but the method is essentially the same and has stood up to centuries of trial. Venice stands on a forest of oak piles driven into the lagoon bed. New work also uses oak piles driven five or six metres deep and backed by ferro-concrete *palancole.* In the city, when the work is completed, the pavement is re-laid in the traditional way. The characteristic oblong slabs of stone called *maccini* are nowadays cut from trachite which is brought from the Montegrotto Terme in the Euganean Hills near Padua. They are laid on a bed of sand and water and then battered in. A mixture of liquid sand and cement is then poured over them and the edges marked off with strips of metal.

A simpler, more rustic effect was needed in the islands and also a less expensive one. The task here too was enormous. At the island of Vignole one and a half kilometres of stone-faced sea walls were built, at the Lido some six hundred metres, at Mazzorbo six hundred and fifty metres, at Torcello the whole island, at Burano one and a half kilometres and, in addition, there were all the interior canals to be renovated. At Torcello the system used in the canals was to drive long oak stakes, which in these days are brought mostly from France, into the bed of the canal and to ram coarse gravel behind the wall of stakes to keep the soil in place. In the lagoon brick is often used to face the quays with a finish of Istrian stone. Here the path along the canal is of herring-bone brick specially chosen to stand up to the heavy tourist foot traffic, the damp and the sudden changes in winter temperatures. Along the fields which lie beside the lagoon are piled large chunks of stone which serve to break the wash of motor-boats and so protect the land from erosion. In Torcello there is also a good example of the close working co-operation between the Soprintendenza ai Monumenti and the Genio Civile (the civil engineering authority). There was a sea wall some hundred yards long at the Cà S. Tomà which dated from the seventeenth century and which had fallen into considerable disrepair. The stone was removed, new foundations of ferro-concrete were laid below water level and the best stone relaid with new dressed Istrian stone making up the rest. The result was a beautiful piece of engineering and an admirable piece of restoration.

The most rustic renovation is to be seen in the island of S. Francesco del Deserto which has now been almost entirely surrounded by new earth banks planted with cypresses. This method is in harmony with the gardens and orchards of the monastery. The most immediately obvious renovation is along the main Mazzorbo canal. On the inhabited side a broad pavement abuts on a little brick wall topped with dressed stone. On the other side the fields and vineyards are protected from the wash, which is considerable in the broad canal which carries a great deal of heavy traffic, by large rough-hewn stone blocks which break the impact of the waves.

The island of Burano has undergone the most complete restoration. The coasts facing on to the wide canals which surround the island are defended by the usual method of *palancole* and *pali* topped off by little brick walls with a stone finish. The interior canals, which are subject to very little wash, are lined with oak *pali*. At intervals there are *scivoli* or ramps for drawing up boats, and *scaletti di ormeggio* or little steps leading down to mooring points. These are all of brick. There are also three *darsene* or little ports for fishing vessels. Nearly all round the island there is a quay paved with porphyry brought down from the mountains behind Trento.

The Venetian Republic took all possible precautions to make the lagoon a place to live in. After many years of neglect and inertia this concept was endangered. Perhaps the most encouraging things to come out of the disastrous floods of November 1966 were sufficient money, allied to a new interest throughout the world in the protection of the environment, and, in Italy, a growing social consciousness. Thanks to the former the engineers and scientists doing basic research on the movements of masses of water and subsidence of the lagoon bed can go ahead with the work of the physical protection of the lagoon. Thanks to the persistence of the people of the lagoon it will, perhaps, remain a place to live in.

It will be a different place from that described hitherto, because though tradition in the lagoon is strong the forces of change in this century are stronger. This book does not pretend to study all the communities in the lagoon because most of them have lost the flavour of societies in their own right. In Murano, for instance, proximity to Venice has tended to wash out individual traits. Other settlements, such as Pellestrina or S. Pietro in Volta, are dormitory communities too small to keep alive a sense of difference, pivoting rather on the place of work than the home community. Other islands are abandoned, inhabited only intermittently or occupied by hospitals and other institutions which cannot be regarded as societies. So we shall be concerned with Burano, a valid society because sufficiently remote still to possess a sense of being different while being a community and yet under great pressure to conform to current standards, together with the islands of Torcello, Santa Cristina and S. Francesco del Deserto which are strongly attracted into the orbit of Burano's vitality and which demonstrate stages of change and decay in the traditional lagoon communities. As much as possible the

13

people of these islands have been left to speak for themselves. The tapes have been edited only to avoid repetition and reduce diffuseness. The aim has been to preserve as much as possible in translation the individual tone of voice.

2 Burano—An Island Community

The origins of Burano are disputed. The most widely held view among historians is that the original settlement, which ancient writers called Burano-on-the-Sea and which lay much closer to the lines of dunes which close the northern lagoon from the Adriatic Sea than does the present community, was founded by refugees from Altino when that flourishing city was overrun by barbarians. Other historians claim that the people were coaxed away from the heresy propagated by the Lombards who had, indeed, been invading hordes in their time but whose influence for evil had become spiritual rather than material or military. The first settlement is said to have taken its name from the Porta Boreana (or North Gate) of Altino. Other historians, while not disputing that the refugees came from Altino, aver that this city was founded by a much older civilisation than the Roman (which they rather disparage) and may well have had its origin in some Greek colony. They point to pre-Roman vestiges of port establishments for sea-going vessels in Altino and in some of the lagoon islands. With academic venom one authority accuses a mafia of archaeologists of refusing to take into account evidence of pre-Roman occupation. and even going so far as to bury it again if inadvertently dug up.

There is certainly a strong tradition that the Buranelli are different, at least among those who dislike them. This includes most of the inhabitants of the other islands of the lagoon and the neighbouring *terraferma*. This is a two-way traffic of dislike based on a long-established economic rivalry as well as local chauvinism and is returned by the Buranelli with equal passion. So, you will often hear it said that the Buranelli are orientals, that 'they are not like us', that they have dark sallow skins and un-Italian tightly curled hair. They are probably, some will say, descended from a tribe that came from Asia Minor or, say others, more likely descended from the galley-slaves quartered in Burano when not wanted in the Venetian wars. Their language points to a different origin, full, as it is, of many words unknown in any other Venetian dialect. They are devious and terrible thieves. As one man said to me: 'Yes, of course a Venetian will steal, but with remorse. A Buranello would only be filled with remorse if he missed an opportunity to steal.'

Even Horatio Brown, an acute and usually affectionate observer, said:

> The men of Burano have not a good reputation; and probably, if a collision occurs in the small canals of Venice, the gondolier will tell you that the offenders are *Buranei*, unless he chooses to fasten the blame on those other aquatic scapegoats, the *Chiozzotti* (men of Chioggia). This evil repute is hereditary. The magistrates of the old Republic found it difficult to preserve order among the women of Burano, who held their market in Venice, near their landing place on the Fondamenta Nuova, and used to set the quarter by the ears with their quarrels.

Another man told me: 'The Buranelli are oriental, devious, a bit untrustworthy but if, if, they accept you they take you to their hearts.'

In this controversy the only point on which I have personal experience is the last. If you are taken to their hearts you have a friend for life. The Buranelli themselves maintain that they did come from Altino. The Torcellani, on the other hand, insist that they could not possibly have done so because they are not peasants. The true descendants of the Altino refugees must be the Torcellani because they are, and they always have been peasants.

However that may be, the island of Burano-on-the-Sea was gradually diminished and drowned by the action of the tides and the currents of the rivers Piave and Sile which ran through deltas in the lagoon to the sea. The unhappy inhabitants had to go cap in hand to the neighbouring settlement of Maiurbium to beg a piece of land on which to resettle.

Once established as a close neighbour of Maiurbium (which later became known as Mazzorbo) the Buranelli set about acquiring that other indispensable adjunct to a stable Venetian community: some saints of their own. To their great satisfaction a sealed stone coffin came aground on the foreshore of Burano. But even the strongest fisherman failed to haul it ashore. Luckily a passing group of innocent little children took up the ropes and, with the greatest of ease, drew the coffin through the settlement to the church. The stone coffin proved to contain the bodies of three saints, S. Albano, S. Domenico and S. Orso, and had been miraculously wafted from the Greek island of Magonza.

At a later date when Torcello had become a vassal of Venice, Burano became part of the administrative area, comprising also Mazzorbo and the now vanished islands of Costanziaca and Ammiana, governed under a *vici* from Torcello on behalf of Venice.

Although Mazzorbo had already lost its chance to become an independent city it was a much more important place than Burano was ever to become. Vittore Carpaccio's family was said to originate from Mazzorbo. The first customs house or *palata* in this part of the lagoon was established there and a number of monasteries bought land and built sumptuous churches and conventual buildings. The last of the great churches of Mazzorbo, S. Giovanni Evangelista, was destroyed in 1810 on the suppression of the monasteries by order of Napoleon. The only remaining church is Santa Caterina, also a convent church and which now serves as the parish church. The destruction of the monasteries heralded a long period of poverty with peasants working the land mostly for absentee landlords.

More interesting for the future development of Burano is the statement made in 1227 that most of the fish sold in Venice came from these islands and also from Chioggia and Poveglia in the southern lagoon. By the end of the fifteenth century the population of Burano had increased sufficiently for it to be required to furnish fifty men to serve in Venetian warships. Burano's brief glimpse of fame came with the birth of Baldassare Galuppi in 1706. He brought to the island, to which he seems to have remained greatly attached, something of the music and polite civilisation of eighteenth-century Venice. But not even the fame or the presence of *Il Buranello* as he was known, could change the tenor of the island's life. It continued to be as it always had been and still is, a simple, independent, poor existence of working people.

Horatio Brown contrasts the people of Mazzorbo and Burano thus:

The natives of Mazzorbo are quiet and gentle, with some of that mild Saturnian sweetness which seems to mingle in the blood of those who deal closely with the earth. They are also singularly beautiful, especially the family at the wineshop. The Buranelli are quick, brusque, rough; with something of the saltness and pungency of the sea on which they live. The streets are noisy and dirty. You will hear plenty of abuse on all sides. The boys are audacious, persistent and tormenting as flies . . . Nor are the Buranelli beautiful as are the people of Mazzorbo, unless it be for a certain sculpturesque cleanness and firmness of limb. Meeting them as they row back from fishing, only a little more clothed than when they came out of the water, ten or twelve boatfuls racing together who shall be first to reach Burano, the sculptor would find many suggestions for the moulding of muscles in play. Or, again, one may see them, a long line of six or seven men, towing the heavy barges, laden with lagoon mud that goes to fertilise the fields round Pordenone. They all bend with a will to the ropes, splashing through the shallow water at the side of the canal . . . There is something fine and bronze-like about the men of Burano, and they have, to counter-balance their evil repute, the fame of doing more work for less pay than any of the islanders of the lagoons. The men are chiefly engaged in fishing and in towing; and the women are not idle, though the noise they make would lead a stranger to think so.

During some hundreds of years the action of the tides and currents and the defensive measures against them considerably changed the pattern of water move-ments and consequently of land masses. Many islands were either eaten away by the tides and abandoned or, as was the case with Mazzorbo and Torcello, became silted up. The consequences of this were disastrous. Stagnant water brought mosquitoes which brought malaria or *la febbre* as they still call it or *la miasma palustre* (marsh miasma) as earlier writers called it. Burano alone escaped and seems to have been continuously and healthily inhabited since its foundation. The people will tell you that the reason for this is that Burano is surrounded on all sides by wide, fast-flowing, tidal canals. Burano has suffered very severely in the past from the diseases of overcrowding and poverty, diseases such as tuberculosis and malnutrition, but it has not suffered the debilitating effects of constant fever. Life in the island has, to this extent, been healthy in spite of the shortage of fresh water. There are no springs in Burano. In the old days there were only wells which were brackish at best and fetid at worst. Some fifteen years ago this situation was put right by running a pipeline form the hills behind Venice across the lagoon to Burano and the mainland beyond. This brings a good supply of excellent water which has been piped to all the houses and has put an end to the old jibe of Burano's ill-wishers that they have clean houses and dirty persons.

The great change in Burano's life came with the prosperity of the 1960s combined with an improved *vaporetto* service which enabled the islanders to take advantage of new and more jobs. The last war seems to have made few changes and left few impressions. Men of military age served, strangely enough for this maritime people, mostly in the army, as they mostly still do for their military service. They seem to have endured their army years passively and without much interest. One bomb was dropped on the island and killed eleven people. Italian, and later German, troops garrisoned a nearby fort. If you talk to the fishermen they will tell you, still in low, shocked tones, how, when they were out in their *sandoli,* they used to hear the shots when the partisans were executed on the abandoned island of Madonna del Monte just before the new cut in Mazzorbo. One of them said to me: 'If you watch when you are on the *vaporetto* you will see some of the older men who remember cross themselves as they pass the island. I always do. What a wicked thing that was!'

The aspect of the island has changed very little over the years. Burano has always been crowded and the little cottages squat side by side and back to back in every possible space. At most points there is a quay or space to haul up a boat round the coast of the island which is intersected by several canals with innumerable elbows and crowded with moored boats. The larger fishing boats, the *bragoze,* are usually moored in the new little port, the one beside the *casa del pescatore* (fishermen's co-operative). There are several wooden bridges but only one brick and stone bridge which links the Quay of the Assassins to the opposite side near the Calle dei Saladi, the Calle Larga is the main shopping street and leads to the Piazza at the top with the church of St. Martin, the municipal *palazzo,* the house where Baldassare Galuppi was born and the elegant little building which used to house the lace-school.

The houses are very small. Usually there is one large room at street level divided into a kitchen and a living space, sometimes by an arch. Access to the house is straight into this room and whenever possible the door is kept open for light and air, though in summer the opening is protected by an awning if it gets the full sun. The stairs, which are usually stone or tiled, rise without bannisters out of this room. Above, there are one or two bedrooms with sometimes a third in the loft if there is head-room. Space for a little bathroom or shower and lavatory will have been found upstairs or sometimes under the stairs. Everything is bright and clean.

Since there is so little space inside, the *calle* or the quay on which the house stands is appropriated and, as a result, swept and garnished like the house. Here, in the poorer

houses, still without a washing machine, the housewife or her daughter will thump the washing on a board in a tub. It is then hung out across the *calle* on a line on a tall prop so that people can pass, dodging the drips, or slung along the facade from window to window. Small things are put on little racks beside the front door. At mealtimes the iron charcoal grill is

21

lit and put out in the *calle* and, whenever the weather permits, a low chair is placed on the shady side for anybody with a minute to spare. There are few houses with more than two storeys and a few with stone facings and wrought-iron balconies but the differences in size and style are not great and do not give the lie to the proud statement: 'We do not have any *signori* (gentry) nor any paupers' in Burano.

The quickest way to gain an idea of Burano as a community is to stand at the top of the ramp at the *vaporetto* landing stage at low tide, when it tilts sharply downwards, as the evening *motonave* (the large ship carrying some thousand passengers) brings the main body of workers home to Burano.

The space behind you has been occupied all the afternoon, at least in the good weather, by groups of little chairs where the women, their housework done, the evening meal bought and prepared, the little children fetched from the kinder-garten run by the nuns round the corner, sit and gossip and make lace or sew or embroider or knit or string beads with a sort of little besom broom made of fine, long, flexible steel needles which they prod into a pile of beads in a tray balanced on their knees and in no time at all make long snaky skeins of beads which are later cut into lengths for necklaces. Little children cavort about on their tricycles and bigger ones play variants on the cops and robbers theme, brandishing pistols and cannoning off the legs of grown-ups who swipe at them ineffectually and without much real intention of making contact.

The first sign of the homecoming ship is usually not the ship at all, although one can see the mast sticking up over the trees and houses as it makes its way along the Mazzorbo canal, but the fast walkers who have left the *motonave* at Mazzorbo and come briskly along the path which skirts the old cemetery, over the wooden bridge to Burano, and who disperse to their homes on that side of the island. Then the *motonave* swings with somewhat ponderous majesty round the curve and moors alongside.

If, at that stage, you glance behind you, you will find the place deserted. The little chairs, one holding knitting and another the lace-cushion, one for sitting on and one for use

as a footstool, stand in groups like children at a party waiting for something to happen. The women have disappeared
indoors to lay the tables, scrub the children's faces and put
the finishing touches to the meal so that all shall be ready
when the men come home. It is one of the points which mark
off the day. With the return of the men and the girls with jobs
away from Burano the tempo changes.

If you look back to the *motonave*, bulky like a
Mississippi paddle-steamer and flat-bottomed to negotiate
the lagoon channels at low water, you will see the crowd
edging towards the side as she ties up. As they start coming
up the ramp you, from your point of vantage, will chiefly see
a sea of faces. All the types of Burano are among them in
their neat shirts and pullovers, for, as always in Venice, they
have changed out of their working clothes since leaving their
furnaces, offices and bars. Suits are rare and usually the only
uniforms seen are worn by the *marinai* of the *vaporetto*
service and the occasional soldier on leave. They are all in a
hurry and hungry and want to get home. Their very early
breakfast had been small and since then they have only had a
snack from their lunch-tin. It is a fairly noisy occasion: greetings, quips, comradely insults and sometimes more serious
ones fly about. The wave proceeds like a bore taking a tide
up a river and disperses in back-waters and *calli* and
campielli and *cortili*, and doors are closed or, in summer, the
awning is twitched into place and for an hour or so
peacefulness descends on Burano. It is one of the few quiet
times of the day.

The journey on the *motonave* has been far from quiet. For
the men and girls working outside Burano the *motonave*
serves the purpose of the village well as in the old days: a place
where you have to go, where everyone goes and which,
because of this fact, becomes a meeting place. As the ship
fills up small groups form, loosely linked with neighbouring
groups, and the conversation veers from a tight, argumenta-
tive discussion within a group to disparate talk in which
other groups join. Nearly all the men have an open newspaper in their hands which they read in only the most desul-
tory way. The younger men and the boys have story books
in illustrated strips and some spell out goggle-eyed the latest

23

adventures of characters of international renown such ·as Batman. The bar (which is usually closed in recognition of being a tourist facility) is where the serious men congregate, usually to play cards. Four players spread a newspaper over their knees to act as a table and friends sitting on the back-to-back benches bend over to watch the play with concentration, muttering, grimacing and taking an earnest part in each post mortem. The games are played with Trevigiane packs, which are long and thin and colourful and in many ways resemble tarot cards. There are four suits — *spade* (swords), *coppe* (goblets), *denari* (pennies) and *bastoni* (sticks). The court cards in each suit are *il re* (the king), *il cavallo* (the horse) and *la vecchia* (the old one) and the other cards often carry scoring values different from their face markings. The games most usually indulged in on the *vaporetto* are *sancagna* and *madrasso;* both of them are played on the basis of taking tricks and have complicated scoring rules. The play is usually for drinks which are consumed with lightning rapidity in the bar of the *vaporetto* station, partly in order to get home to dinner quickly and partly because it seems to be an Italian habit to down one's drink in a bar with a speed which indicates that it is the lift rather than the taste which counts. Girls and little boys play a milder version of these games called *la scopa*, which is a simplified form of whist.

If, for the men, the half-hour or so between Murano, where most of them come on board, and Burano, is relaxation, a social occasion ranking with the evening stroll up and down the Via Baldassare Galuppi and round the *piazza* and the eternal sitting about in cafés and at the pavement tables outside them, then for the girls it is an opportunity to get on with their knitting or needlework. It is an almost frightening display of industry, almost mindless in its relentless application, and it is accompanied by constant talk. Almost anything that can be conveniently carried is likely to be made on the *vaporetto* but there does seem to be a rough classification of objects by age. The young girls make things to wear themselves; those embarking on marriage embroider endless table-cloths and pillow cases with their young men sitting stolidly beside them; young mothers knit baby garments and older mothers knit pullovers of all sizes and sew summer dresses for daughters; grannies are back on the bootee, baby jacket routine. The occasional idle hands only intensify the dizziness induced by all these clacking tongues and clicking fingers. The only rest for one's eyes and ears is provided by the newly-in-love, and one cannot with any kindness look at them, suffering as they do under the battery of the curious glances of a closed, inquisitive society.

All day the women, the old people and the children have had Burano to themselves. The life of the women, in particular, has greatly changed with the prosperity of recent years. It has taken the harshness out of their lives. Earlier, they went out to work if they could, because any addition, however small or irregular, to the family purse made all the difference between want and just making ends meet. It was mostly the girls and unmarried women who went out to work and mostly as domestic servants, for there were few opportunities for untrained women such as now exist, for instance, in the glass factories. The married women were invariably drudging at home among their innumerable babies. Now the increase in wages and security of employment (for as long as they may last in a period of increasing economic difficulties) have relieved many of them of the need to work outside the home, as in the rest of Italy where the percentage of women working has gone down since the beginning of the century from about thirty per cent to a little less than twenty per cent. This trend may well be reversed if wages do not keep pace with the cost of living or if more opportunities for the employment of married women were created by more, and more varied, industrialisation. At present the married women in Burano who wish to work often run little shops or help their husbands in family businesses, like that well-known bar-lady who is the same shape behind and before, with the only difference that in front it is a little higher up, and who greatly enjoys the uproarious repartee she delights in provoking. Families, too, are smaller now, which has relieved the women of the unremitting toil of caring for a tribe of small children with little means and primitive equipment. If one compares the women who have grown up during the last fifteen years of prosperity with those only ten years older, one sees, at once, the difference made by less child-bearing and less hard work. They have retained their youth, their looks, their figures. They have a resilience, a bounce, which their elders lost over a wash-tub or a sink long ago. Women's lives were grim before and perhaps *la mamma's* standing in the family is a recognition of her hard work and sacrifice. At least, her life, unlike that of her modern suburban counterpart in most of the great residential conurbations of the world, was not lonely. The men were often away at work but in those days the chief occupation was fishing, which is seasonal and further governed by tides so that the fisherman is often at home, even if busy mending nets or cleaning out the boat. The phenomenon of loneliness does not exist in a small society where you went through school with the woman next door and next door to that, though that may not make you like them any better. The young Burano housewife of today no longer has a communal meeting place or gossip point since water has been piped to the houses and she no longer has to fetch it from a standpipe in the *cortile* or *calle*. Then the constant to-ing and fro-ing with buckets provided a link with the world. Now shopping seems to have taken its place.

Shopping is generally done for one meal only. It is a habit left over from the past when money was so short and so uncertain that only the minimum was spent at any time in case a greater need — illness, losing the fishing nets or the expense of a funeral — pre-empted the rest. The woman still goes out to buy an *etto* of ham here, two eggs there, a roll of bread for each member of the family, a packet of spaghetti, a small tin of this and a snippet of that. This domestic chore of buying the dinner is accompanied by an exchange of news and views with a sharp glance into that neighbour's windows and the other's washing, on an intricate network of routes that includes all the relatives, the in-laws, any subjects particularly gossip-worthy as well as the relevant shops.

There are very many small shops in Burano and, although they are already too many to be economically viable, they seem to be increasing in number. In 1972 the Italian national average was one food shop for one hundred and ten inhabitants. The only explanation for this proliferation which suggests itself is that a little shop is a convenient outlet for the woman of the family and does bring in a little money. Then the shop becomes a part of that complex of jobs, perhaps six or seven in a family of four wage-earners, which together add up to a reasonable livelihood for the family. This amateur competition makes it more difficult for the professional to make a living at all. As one excellent craftsman said:

I am the only trained shoemaker in Burano. The population is nearly 6,000 and you would think that one could make a living. But I do not seem to be able to. I have been mending shoes here for fifteen years and now I am looking for some other place to work. I had thought of going to Murano. It is a big place and there is no shoemaker there but I do not care for Murano. They have their knife into foreigners, talk about *campanilismo* (parochialism). They are five kilometres away and they treat us Buranelli as foreigners.

I am a craftsman and was taught by my father how to make shoes. But I haven't made a single pair of shoes in the fifteen years I have been at it. People buy rubbish made of plastic because it costs 200 lire less than a pair of leather shoes. Look at him (pointing at a customer), fudged with money (loud protests from customer) and look at the muck he brings me to mend. He could pay to have a good pair of shoes made to measure which would last him years if he looked after them. There is very little satisfaction in the work these days, and very little money.

Another problem is that everybody thinks they can mend shoes. All the old men who retire on a small pension or who have got a disability pension set up as shoemakers. There would be work here for one man. I could feed my family if I were the only shoemaker here but I cannot do so if these self-styled shoemakers take away my trade.

Life is lived publicly in all hot countries, particularly in the poorer areas. In a congested island like Burano it is even more public. There is no escaping the inquisitive eye, the nose sniffing for gossip. The conditions of life in Burano are such that people are constantly, necessarily inevitably looking over each other's shoulders all the time. Everybody knows everybody else's business and the prevailing habit of shouting all the time, as everywhere in the south, removes any stigma of poking your nose into other people's business. If you quarrel with your wife or if your daughter flounces out of the house, everybody knows. If you clout your child the priest will probably comment on it, if you leave your husband's pants undarned your neighbour will know, since there is nowhere but the *calle* to hang them out to dry. It is no doubt this continuous scrutiny which has made the Buranelli so houseproud. Practically the only defence you have is to make sure that your house is at all times spick and span and ready to receive the most censorious visitor. All this demands a great deal of work and self-discipline constantly to present a good front to the world. You cannot afford to be caught out if you are out to catch others and all the Buranelli seem to live simultaneously on both sides of this fence.

Yet it would be wrong to think that this houseproud attitude is only for show. There is, in Burano, a real care for cleanliness. They are not only good and careful housewives, they are energetic too. In the early mornings you will find them scrubbing and polishing and even sweeping the quay or the *calle* in front of their houses. When all is clean and tidy they leave the door open, partly to let air and light into these tiny houses, partly to show the neighbours that the job has been properly done, that they have nothing to hide. If the housewife then trots off to do her shopping in driblets, three or four times when once would have done, this is a legitimate moment of relaxation in an active life. When she returns she will clean her fish on a paper on the doorstep or the edge of the canal or convenient block of stone and prepare her charcoal stove and, when the time comes, clap her fish in the wire holders and leave it cooking in the *calle* within convenient sight of whatever she is doing in the house.

In the old days all the cooking was done on charcoal and since it had to be bought it was used as sparingly as possible. So the cooking was quick. Fish is traditionally grilled or fried and the *polenta* (a stiff maize porridge) cooked on an iron sheet or flat pan. Now stoves are fired by bottled gas but the cooking has not changed and the oven is seldom used. Those few women who still make their own *busolai* are still more likely to take it round to the bakery to be cooked when the bread has been removed than to put it into their own ovens at home. There is no tradition of making bread in the home. Indeed bread did not become a staple part of the diet until quite recently. *Polenta* traditionally and still today is the daily fare in most families though now, except in the very poorest homes, there is bread on the table as well.

The Buranelli enjoy their food, even if the range is rather limited, and the women take great pains with the cooking as this exchange shows:

Housewife: Families have their special tastes, one likes broth, another *polenta*, another fish according to their tastes. In our family we particularly like *zucchini al forno* . . .
Friend: *Zucchini?* What rubbish, you mean *succhette* . .
Housewife: You shut up. We are talking Italian. In Italian you don't say *succhette*. You say *zucchini*. You don't know anything. *Zucchini*, very little marrows done in the oven. Lovely! We are also very fond of stuffed tomatoes in

29

our family. Burano is very famous for its fish — straight out of the water it comes on to our charcoal grills. You have probably seen our little charcoal grills in the *calli* outside the doors. We clap the cleaned fish into a wire holder and put it over the charcoal and it is very good. We usually eat it with *polenta*. Excellent! Then in Burano we are also very well-known for a biscuit which we call *busolai buranelli*. They are made by mixing as much flour as sugar and a great many eggs and when you have mixed it all into a dough you shape it into rings and take it along to the baker and he puts it into the oven after he has taken the bread out and leaves it for a long time. It must cook very slowly. They are very rich.

After the mid-day meal has been cleared away and the children have gone off to play, the woman of the house may, for an hour or so, take her little chair and her lace-making cushion and join one of the small groups of women working in shady corners or under the trees. If she lives far from these traditional meeting places she will sit alone on the shady side of the *calle* making her lace until it is time to prepare the evening meal before the wage-earners return home on the *motonave*.

If the wife is proud of the inside of the house, the husband is equally so of the outside. When the colour-wash of the house begins to look a little shabby or faded the man of the house will go out and buy a bag of colour and furbish up his brushes. As one of them said:

We Buranelli are very competitive people and in the spring you will see first one and then another house-owner preparing to make his house beautiful. Each one chooses the colour he fancies and it can cost quite a lot to make a good job of a house. At one time the Soprintendenza ai Monumenti tried to give advice about colours and impose what they called a harmonious colour scheme. They even offered free distemper. But we would not have it. We did not want a harmonious colour scheme. We were not offered the colours we wanted so we refused them. We did not want free colour-wash and we didn't want any advice either. We wanted to do it our way. They said we would get into trouble if we didn't do as we were told. So now we colour-wash our houses very early in the morning before the police come round and then they can't say anything because it is all finished and not a paint brush in sight. Painting? Who's been painting? Nobody has been painting here. The house was blue yesterday and now it is a lovely peach. I wonder however it got like that! Of course we ought not to behave like this but we all do. Each of us does his house his own way and the result is very artistic, very fine, don't you think? It costs a lot nowadays to paint the house every year but if one starts the others follow because they want to go one better!

The Buranelli want to do things as they want in more ways than colourwashing their houses. They are independent people and their competitiveness is a reflection of this, as perhaps their secretiveness about their affairs is an aspect of the public living forced on them by conditions. They keep themselves to themselves which seems everywhere to go along with keeping up with the Joneses.

With the rise of wages in the 1960s their competitive spirit acquired a new vigour. Refrigerators, washing machines, television sets, telephones, bathrooms (two or three houses in Burano now even have two bathrooms and one wonders how they found room for them), bedroom suites, tricycles, settees and armchairs, a new boat, a bigger outboard engine, more glorious weddings and more expensive funerals proliferated. But the chief pride and glory was the house. The new prosperity turned a community of tenants into a community of house-owners. One of them told me:

After the war rents were controlled and things got a bit difficult for the landlords, just at a time when they could expect to make more money out of the tenants because wages were going up. So the owners wanted to sell out at a time when the tenants had money coming in for the first time in their lives. And most of them bought the houses they were living in. It was really the women of Burano who did it, especially the mothers. A family that had a father and two or three children earning could find the money to buy the house, even if they did not have much

31

put by. But they only put the money into buying the house if the mother made them. Now the value of the houses has greatly increased and families are very pleased that they own their houses. It is the women who did it, mainly the mothers.

The steel which binds together the community of Burano is the mother, *la mamma*, and she guides, governs, cajoles and sometimes bullies, and always adores the family. If Burano became, because of better pay, conditions and range of employment, a consumer society, it remained a solid, coherent, vital community because of *la mamma*. She continues as a sort of emotional pole providing both stability and continuity. There are grown men working abroad who telephone to *la mamma* every other Sunday. She maintains the traditions but she also belts her boys and girls into the twenty-first century — more education, better jobs, status, mind your manners, always take off your shoes before you go upstairs, don't waste your money, change your shirt. She is the embodiment of what you might call the *nostrani* (our own produce) syndrome in human terms. If *nostrani* artichokes and fish are better than other people's then it follows that the people must be better too. *La mamma* knows that they are and has every intention that they shall remain so.

You can see *la mamma's* hand in the number of marriages within the Burano community. It is not only a matter of marrying the girl next door, though in such a closed society the opportunities for meeting potential marriage partners — on the *vaporetto*, in the constant to-ing and fro-ing in the *calli*, in the evening stroll in the *piazza* — are much greater than during the pressure of working hours or the hustle to catch the boat home. It is also *la mamma's* care to keep the family together, to build its alliances, to increase its standing, to frown on the pretensions of the slut or the sluggard or the ne'er-do-well to enter the fold, and to keep them all under her protective wing. *La mamma* is upset and preoccupied if she cannot see her young every day, to watch over their health and happiness. This deep and all-embracing affection does not end when her young found their own families. There is a ring of approval in the mother who said:

We Buranelli like to marry here in Burano. Some of the young ones who work outside meet people from other places like Treporti or Murano. They do also sometimes meet on holidays, jaunts on saints' days, factory outings and so on. But mostly marriages are made in Burano, in the island, among our own people. We like it that way.

There is a certain hankering after romantic marriages fostered by the novelettes they read and films and television, but the harsh past casts a long shadow and when the time comes to make a decision both partners still seem to look for the qualities of tenacity, endurance and persistence which will serve in hard times and penury. In the meantime the girls, guided by *la mamma*, save and stitch and knit against their marriage. It is no longer quite a question of a dowry but tending to the same end. Traditionally in Torcello it is the bridegroom who buys the bedroom furniture, in Burano it is the bride, but more and more 'both sides do the house. You put in what you have. Sometimes it is half and half. Whoever has more puts in more. My wife and I arranged things this way, but then of course we were both working and bringing in good money. Maybe earlier the women had a dowry but now they make up their own if they can'.

If the matriarchal influence is still acceptable it is partly a reflection of a widespread Mediterranean, perhaps Catholic, cult of the mother, but also because her role is still a useful one, in a way that the small biological family unit of highly industrialised societies is tending to forget and the women's lib movements actively to eliminate. It is also partly because of *la mamma*'s own quality and toleration. Burano voted sixty-two percent in favour of divorce, a figure which reflects an attitude of mind and not an actual pressing need as the present divorce rate is extremely low. It is also that children are very highly regarded in the family and *la mamma*'s experience and help is much prized. The parents and grandparents, indeed the whole wide family, are still of overriding importance in bringing up the children. There has been no delegation of this responsibility to the schools, perhaps because the school age does not start till a child is six

33

(though they very often go to a kindergarten earlier) and because the school year is so short. Whatever the reason the basic training for how to behave in the family and the community and what sort of person to aim to become is given in the home. You tell the truth, you are courteous, you say 'Buon giorno' and shake hands with visitors from the earliest age. If you do something really wicked in this congested island an uncle or aunt or an older cousin is bound to see. They will not wait to tell your father, they will give you a dressing-down or a clout right away. At the same time the love and affection which surrounds and supports them (and which in their teens they may find oppressive) gives them a confidence and an openness which is a pleasure to see.

La mamma's role in preserving a traditional way of life has been greatly helped by the strength of family feeling in Italy and by the geographical isolation of Burano. Both are weaker than they were. There are now visible the first tiny cracks in the dykes which protect the family and which are bound to widen in time and bring the disintegration of the family, lamented in many societies today. The prosperity of recent years has loosened the tight bonds of the family. In times of poverty and strain it is a comfort to have the support and sympathy of an extended family network. When social services are poor or non-existent (and Italy is not a rich society) family support is essential. If a member of a family is taken to hospital, even today, the aunts and cousins and women in-laws make daily visits, to help with nursing and feeding the invalid as well as looking after those who have been left at home. All poor societies have to hang together to survive. Burano has always been a community of poor people, discounted and neglected. It is still discounted and neglected but for the last fifteen years it has not been so poor. Fifteen years is too short a time to destroy an essential need of centuries and if a strong family spirit continues to exist it is partly due to the memory of bitter penury. Nobody helped them. They had to help one another. Burano was an over-populated urban slum even if it stood in the wide stretches of the lagoon. Urban slums are not romantic in the way that rural slums are sometimes thought to be. In an urban slum there are no roses round the cottage door. There is just a stench of overcrowded humanity. If conditions have improved — and they have improved out of all recognition — the Buranelli feel that they have done it all themselves. Burano does not feel that it owes anybody anything. The Buranelli pulled themselves up by their own bootstraps and it is a matter of dour pride that this should be so. They owe it to the sturdy independence and toughmindedness bred by generations of fishermen and boatmen. The family is the core of the extraordinary tight-knit society which they built for their own protection. It is a society which looks after its own but this is not to say that it is not a rough society. As one of the women said:

'Mistakes' are usually put in an orphanage. Sometimes the grandparents take in illegitimate children but not often. They are taken in charge by the *Infanza Abandonata* and the state pays. Orphans are different. They are closer, dearer to the families and usually they are taken in by somebody, grandparents, uncles, aunts. They love them and don't want them to go away into orphanages. When I was a young married woman we had the six children of my brother living with us. *Dio mio,* that was a difficult time. I had two and another one coming and that winter we only had *polenta* and dried figs to eat. Naturally with that sort of food the children were constantly upset and some became really ill on top of everything else.

One of the foundlings told me this about his early days:

I should explain that my personal situation is a bit ambiguous. You see . . . how shall I say . . . well, I can only say that from the time I was quite small I was in the family of my foster mother and father. They were not my real parents, you understand, but they were good to me and I loved them sincerely and I called them *mamma* and *papa* and, in short, they treated me well, even if they were not my parents and, goodness knows, it was so much better for me to be with them than in an orphanage. But I cannot say that I had a good start in life. Putting aside the fact that I never knew who my mother and father were and, of course, everybody knew about me when I was little and it was so difficult, you can't think how difficult it was and how I used to cry, but at least I have always tried in a small, modest way to be a good citizen and face as best I could the difficulties of my situation. But I suffered, I can tell you, from not having what all the other children had. I always fixed my thoughts on the future when I hoped things would be better and tried to develop some fortitude to face the vicissitudes of my life. Of course I had moments of depression, especially when I was young and hadn't the experience or, if you like, I hadn't developed the philosophy that comes with the years.

Many hurtful things must have been said to him. There are always people ready to trample on others' toes and there are perhaps more of them in a community as up against adversity as Burano used to be. You had to grow a tough carapace to protect your tenderer spots against outrageous fortune. Perhaps this streak of cruelty is even useful in promoting its growth. Recently a group of women making lace under a tree were amusing themselves teaching a little boy aged about four years old to give his surname as *Putana* (whore) and it was found very funny by all except the little boy who, in spite of the sincerity and trust so touching in the very young, was beginning to suspect, with infinite embarrassment, that there was something wrong with what he had been taught: a first harsh lesson that grown-ups were not be trusted. Yet there is in Burano a rough tolerance for departures from the norms of behaviour accepted by society, bred, no doubt, by the close texture of the community, rather as, in earlier periods in England, a man might clout a younger brother for seducing the village girls but be fond of him just the same. In Burano they cheerfully admit divergences 'even though', as they say, 'it is a small place.' 'Until recently we slept ten or twelve in a room and mostly in the same bed, so what can you expect?' What, indeed?

Apart from such, after all, fairly rare cases, Burano continues to care for itself as a community and for its dependants whether very old or very young. In this hermetic, isolated society one would have thought that the old would have played a greater part in maintaining its identity. So much of civilisation is transmitted by the tales of old people. If we have been at all lucky in the old people we have known we have acquired an intimate, if haphazard, knowledge of an earlier society which gives us, however little we may consciously recognise it, a basis of understanding and a point of comparison with the one we ourselves live in and, according to our nature, we can judge how much we have progressed or how far we have fallen from a set of rather shadowy standards. The tales of old people in most societies are the beginning of a sense of history, of some idea of how we have become what we are. If a civilisation is an expression of a society it is usually the memories of the old which provide a sense of continuity. It is curious that this almost universal development seems to be true only to a very limited extent in Burano. This may be because of the dominant position of *la mamma*. When she resigns her onerous duties to her daughters or sons' wives she seems to lay them down altogether and sits contentedly in the *calle* chatting to other abdicated mothers. It may also be because of the restricted nature of the experience of the old. They have been closed within a limited dialect which still varies in many ways from the Venetian spoken in Venice and isolated by distance and the lagoon from contacts except on rare festive occasions. They have a rich recollection of their own island community, and the men an intimate and vivid re-collection of the lagoon and the skills and hazards of navigation and fishing. This was vital lore in earning a living and it remained valid because, until the outboard motor became available at reasonable prices in the 1960s, methods of propelling boats and fishing had not changed for hundreds of years. So what the Buranelli received from the old was the handing down of a skill rather than of a culture. There is no sense of a continuing indentity enshrined in tales or legends specifically Buranelli. Also, and this is to use the word culture in a narrower sense, there seems to be no memory in Burano of the great days of the Serene Republic, of the crowded ecclesiastical life of the eastern lagoon. Baldassare Galuppi's music was never played in the church until an outside influence recently introduced it. There are songs and the old people can be persuaded to sing them in fluty cracked

37

voices but they usually turn out to be the run of Venetian popular songs. The continuing element of cohesion of the community and the *raison d'être* of its identity must be sought elsewhere.

The leit-motif of the recollection of the old is poverty and one comes finally to feel that it was poverty and the insecurity bred of poverty which washed out the recollection of other, gentler aspects of life. The old people of Burano were born to be poor. It had always been like that: there was no other life. You went fishing and you put your little catch into your *sandalo* and you rowed for four hours to the market in Venice and, if you were lucky, you sold it and rowed back for another four hours and when you got home you found you had made barely enough to feed your children on a good day. The poverty of Burano was different from the poverty caused by the depression of the 1930s because it was long-term, ingrained, a normal state of things. It was primary poverty which you could not escape from by any action of your own. It was not a falling-off in a standard of reasonable comfort because you had lost a job which you could hope, one day, to regain. All the way to the horizon there was poverty and the horizon is a long way off in the lagoon. So there is a grimness in the recollections of the old of Burano that does not exist in the memory of, for instance, the peasants of the neighbouring islands. All children in poor or primitive societies are expected to work and work hard but the peasant children also had time to play or were able to turn their work into play. They invented songs and games in the vineyards which served to scare away the birds, which was their allotted job, and it added gaiety and fun to their lives. A fisherboy, out with his father, fished. There was no time for looking about when the tide and the weather set a limit to what you could catch and consequently to what you could earn.

These long centuries of grinding poverty have left their mark on the society. To survive you had to be self-reliant and tough, and so gradually there grew up a community which also became tough, self-reliant, close-knit and in-dependent in order to survive. It is the hundreds of years of adversity which have given Burano the strength to endure

38

while other gentler softer communities nearby were fading away. These characteristics have enabled the community to take the relative prosperity of recent years in its stride and to step in one generation from poverty to a consumer society without toppling over, without losing its old ways or standards or vigour. It has retained its resilience. Now, most of the population leave it daily to earn their living but Burano has not dwindled into a dormitory town. It is a vital community. It may be that the community can only remain strong for as long as it remembers the numbing effects of poverty as the present generation of wage-earners so acutely does. The point of danger, of the loosening of the fabric of the traditional society to the point of disintegration, will come with the maturity of a generation which has not suffered and so cannot remember penury.

The young people of Burano seem to be reacting to their community in one of two ways. They are all of them tending to find the enveloping traditional family, the octopus hug of the family, hampering to their freedom to do and think as they wish. Among the rank and file of not very well-educated, not very intelligent young people this is probably only a temporary state of revolt. They remain deeply attached to the community and may be expected to take their place in it very soon as young fathers and mothers. What they seek is security rather than adventure — which leads one to suppose that they have not entirely forgotten the poverty of the past. The aim of the young men is a good steady job with a pension in the *vaporetto* service or the electricity company or, if their education is sufficient, a clerking job with the municipality. Adventure is something you read about or watch on television. The aim of the girls is marriage to a young man with a steady job. As one young bride said:

My generation did not have to help our parents. My mother had to help hers, of course, but we went to school and when we got home we played. I began working when I was fourteen but the girls who are younger than me have to go on to secondary school before they can begin to work. If you have not learnt a job you go into the glass

39

works to make a bit of money and then you get married. I was trained as a nurse and my husband has a good steady job which will bring in a pension.

These people constitute no danger to the community. This is not the case with the alert, intelligent young people who are beginning to feel that they cannot make their way adequately in the world if they return nightly to an out-of-date, old-fashioned community which gives them no stimulus and no support in pursuit of their ideals, ways of life and professions, which does not allow them to change the society in which they live and frustrates them in their desire to mix with a wider society. These young people are the ones who feel that they must get away, though with a backward glance at the freedom and beauty of the lagoon and a pang at leaving *la mamma*. If they do leave Burano it will be a disaster for the community which cannot flourish if the best are drawn off, though the individuals who leave may go far. A parallel might be drawn here with what R. C. K. Ensor used to say between the wars, that the leadership of the working class in England was being siphoned off by means of scholarships to grammar schools and universities. No community, no class can afford to lose its leaders. If these young people go we may be seeing the last of a vigorous society in Burano.

If, to the old, poverty was what life was about and they are still, personally, very poor and mostly dependent on their children, and if the young people in their various ways are defending themselves from the inadequacies of their society, the children, protected, adored, cossetted, must find Burano a very heaven. Wherever you go in Burano you see children, on Sundays starched and ironed in a way to make an English mother stare, on weekdays comfortably clean and tidy. The whole island is an adventure playground. Boats drawn up out of the water are used as castles, stalking points, pirate ships. Nobody says, 'Don't fall into the canal, dear.' Does anybody ever? One never hears of it happening. Like most of the Mediterranean people they are extremely nice to babies, young mothers allow themselves extraordinarily tender gestures and little boys demonstrate a protectiveness to those younger than themselves with just enough roughness to make the smaller feel bigger and teach him to look after himself. There is a good deal of devilry about and whizzing round corners frightening tourists out of their minds and ringing of doorbells. The doorbells in Burano are placed very high up (you have to stand on a friend) or else so expertly hidden that only the initiated know how to make their presence known. More legitimate games are played in the *piazza* or any wide quay or paved *cortile*. Particularly popular is a variety of deck quoits played with the rubber heels of shoes. These children are the inheritors and one wonders what society they will find when they grow up.

There is a primary school in Burano which also serves the children of Mazzorbo and Torcello and a junior secondary school which all children have to attend to the third class, which means in effect fourteen years of age. Those who go on have to travel to Venice, Padua or Mestre for higher, professional, university and craft training. There are those who will tell you that the Buranelli do not appreciate education and do not press their children to make the most of opportunities now available. This is a sweeping generalisation and against it must be put the very considerable sacrifices and efforts made by an older generation who had their education interrupted, mostly through poverty or some family calamity, to complete the first five years of primary school which was the required term when they were young.

The education service is going through a very difficult period in Italy as in other countries and the teachers' associations have frequent recourse to strike action, which makes the short school year even shorter, as a means of obtaining better pay and conditions. Teachers, primary school teachers in particular, have fallen well behind most skilled workers in salaries. So the schools are closed too often for the well-being of their pupils. On the other hand primary education seems to be a good deal in advance of the secondary and higher levels in teaching methods, nor are they as old-fashioned or as hidebound in their attitudes. Certainly the children learn to read very rapidly. If there is some belittling of the value of education it is partly because the educational process in Italy is a rather dreary, dry-as-dust, academic affair. It is more, however, because Burano has traditionally lived from craftsmanship which you learnt from your father (if, for instance, you intended to become a fisherman) or from some form of apprenticeship (if you went into glass-blowing). There is consequently a very strong tradition towards apprenticeship, the handing down of skills from craftsman to craftsman. Even today young people tend to complete the statutory educational requirements because advance in, and sometimes admission to, most careers is impossible without them or because some specialist knowledge is required (for instance, book-keeping) where the family cannot help. But these are technical requirements. They do not involve such definitions of education as made the United Kingdom Education Act of 1944 famous in its time by specifying that a child should receive an education according to his age, ability and aptitudes. The average Buranello is not interested in this sort of education. He wants to learn as quickly as possible as much as he needs to know to do whatever it is that he wants to do. In his sturdy way he reckons that with hard work and application he will acquire the ability, and as for the aptitudes, he will look after them too.

Education, even of the limited kind the ordinary Buranello will accept, tends to increase the range of available opportunities. Its most obvious influence is on the language which he speaks. The old people speak a variation of Venetian which frequently defeats even an ear acutely attuned to that language. Horatio Brown said of the Buranelli:

> . . . Their dialect is softened almost·to the melting point. In their mouths Venetian, the Ionic of the Italian group of dialects, has been mollified until the ribs of the language, the consonants, are on the verge of disappearing altogether . . . They dwell upon the vowels, redoubling and prolonging them, so that their words seem to have no close, but die away in a kind of sigh. For instance, they call their own town Buraâ, instead of Buran. The effect is not unpleasant, but is rather too sweet and gripless for our northern ears.

The children and young people speak a dialect of a simplified kind and are at home in standard Italian. This is not always true of those who have left school for some time and whose jobs and lives have confined them to Burano. They forget their Italian and their horizons shrink again to the limits of their island. Buranello is the language of the community and the use of Italian except to foreigners and strangers would be regarded as a sign of getting above oneself and would be severely put down. There is no feeling in Burano that their dialect is a bar to communication. This is perhaps because they still live very largely among themselves. Their work, outside Burano, is mostly in the glass factories of Murano and there are enough of them there to make a society of their own even within one which has a very similar mode of speech. The Buranello dialect is in fact one of the pillars on which they build their sense of separateness, their uniqueness, of belonging to a community. Those who do not speak it are outside, foreigners, inferior. Those who have had an opportunity to push on with their studies and find themselves on the brink of higher professional or academic levels have to be very careful, in their general comportment as well as in their language, not to appear to overstep the rest. The people of Burano are intensely proud of all being the same kind of people, with the same background and, in general, the same standard of living. This pride often takes the form: 'There are no *signori* [gentry] here.' Undoubtedly the use of a variant of the Venetian language has been one of the strongest adhesives at work in this close-knit society. The individual can suffer from all this in his career. It is inconceivable that he could remain a member in good standing of the Burano community and, at the same time, a prominent lawyer or politician, a top-ranking civil servant or a doctor with a sophisticated practice. He would have to move away if he succeeded in such professions but not because the Buranelli would not be delighted to use his influence to further their own interests. *La mamma* would be extremely proud of him. The community would regard him as uppity. The conditions of membership include use of the language and staying in line, and they nullify the effect which education should have on the social mobility of the more gifted.

It is the more remarkable that there is no bar imposed by the community to the cultural or intellectual development of individuals. On the contrary, there is an affectionate encouragement to extend the cultural skills and sensibilities which so evidently exist among these people. There is a little orchestra on the island, run entirely on the goodwill of men who have sufficient music in them to make sacrifices to learn an instrument, to maintain the skill they have acquired and to teach it to children who, later, might wish to join the orchestra. There are glass-blowers whose perfection of craftsmanship has an added quality of self-criticism and taste which raises them to the rank of artists. There are wood-carvers, one of whom is frustrated by having to earn his living in another way since sculpture is too uncertain a means of supporting a family. The other seems to keep himself on his work. Both are recognisably artists. There are a number of Sunday painters who show their work, which varies considerably in quality, at the exhibitions which are arranged during the summer months and who are much encouraged by the professional painters who are so often to be seen at work in this attractive place. Intellectual pleasures are less in evidence perhaps because among a people of, on the

44

whole, little education there is not the friendly guidance and smoothing away of difficulties that organisations such as the Workers' Educational Association provided in its heyday in England. Some lectures of this kind are organised occasionally but they seem to be sporadic and undemanding and on the whole are not well-attended unless on subjects startlingly new in a rather old-fashioned community, like relations between the sexes. These had a phenomenal success and provoked heated discussions.

Words, which are the vehicle of ideas, are almost equally neglected though this statement demands immediate correction: Burano is the only place I know where the grocer quietly declaims Dante to himself while slicing up the bacon. But this is a man of outstanding sensibility and intelligence. On the whole Burano is a bookless society. In the little houses you will find cherished pictures, not reproductions or calendars, though you will, of course, find them too, but the personal work of a relative or friend, or a glass object or a framed piece of lace made by one of the family. You will seldom see any books. This may be because their sensibility tends towards the visual, for there are many Buranelli who have a real appreciation of the varying moods of the lagoon and the play of light between the sky and the water. But it would be wrong to exaggerate the incidence of these gifts. The greater part of the population are excellent specimens of the plain, dull, estimable citizenry which comprise the majority of most populations.

Books do not count in their lives in spite of the opportunity for reading afforded by the two forty-minute journeys on the *motonave* going to and from their work. It is only very occasionally that one sees one of these commuters take a book out of his briefcase. A few of the girls read magazines or horoscopes. The men may glance idly at newspapers and one or two sharpen their brains on a crossword puzzle. To some extent this is because reading is not a required skill for most of their jobs and becomes a diminishing skill as their school years recede. It is also partly because books are expensive to buy and not easy to borrow. The public library service is vestigial and housed in the school, which means that it inevitably acquires a schoolmarmish aura and that during the long summer holidays (June to October) it is closed. One young woman said:

> Yes, there is a public library in Burano. It is in the school but it isn't any use. I do not read much. Most of us read papers and weeklies. We don't read many books. I don't look at TV much either. Once I used to get books out of the library but now I don't go any more: I'm married now.

The spoken word is still very important. It not only conveys news and views and the day's happenings. It is the expression of what Richard Hoggart has called 'the fidelity and gentleness of face-to-face working-class communities at their best', to which one might add forbearance and tolerance bred of overcrowded conditions yet combined with an inquisitiveness which almost amounts to the right to know the details of everybody's business. Burano is, in fact, still intensely interested in itself. If you listen to the talk in the cafés and along the quays, if you join a group watching a fisherman sorting his catch, if you wander up and down the *piazza* in the early evening when everyone is out for a stroll, you will find that the talk is all of Burano and its affairs. They do not need television, though most of them have it, because they have one another. A striking instance of this interest in themselves and the community which, together, they compose is the fact that out of the hundreds talked to in collecting material for this book only one declined to talk about himself and his island — and he came from Mestre. For as long as this intense feeling about themselves lasts television seems unlikely, at least among those who grew up in the traditional form of society before it became usual to have a set, to be an over-riding influence on their patterns of behaviour or belief.

They are imitative, but of one another, not following a lead given by television or newspapers. If one buys a dishwasher, the neighbours will seriously discuss buying one to keep abreast. In any case the first one bought it at least as much to get ahead as because he needed it. The spark that led to his buying it was not so much seeing an advertisement (which seems to matter curiously little, as yet, in a society with more money than ever before) as a notion that it would

46

make the neighbours green with envy. If advertisements leave them cold they seem very susceptible to services. The great shopping centres which are springing up in the country-side of the *terraferma* craftily encourage the organisation of bus tours which combine an element of an outing with a shopping spree. Joining one of these outings is a social necessity as well as an economy for the prudent housewife. It is because Burano is so uncommonly self-sufficient that it has been able to resist the blandishments of the television version of the good life and, at the moment, it has reached a point of balance between the solidity of its tradition and the comforts which it thinks worth spending its money on, its own pace-makers setting the tempo and direction of expenditure. It is unlikely to be able to retain its balance on this pinpoint. The young, already resentful at the immobility of their elders in a world spinning with increasing speed, seem much more likely to absorb the message of television and align their expectations and standards on those of the ordinary consumer society.

In cultural matters even more than in others Burano has been neglected. In social matters the norms which apply to the nation apply also here. If pensions, social security or health services are inadequate or dilatory it is because these weaknesses are present in every part of the country. To some extent this applies also to the encouragement of cultural activities. Expenditure on culture tends everywhere to come after social expenditure and this cannot be a source of complaint. Where the difference does become important is that Burano always has been regarded as peripheral not only geographically but in the minds of most. Venetians have a long-established habit of discounting Burano, that remote home of uninteresting working-class people who are of no account. The Venetian willingly concedes that Burano is picturesque. He is delighted to go and eat fish there once or twice in the summer. He does not for one minute consider that its inhabitants have as long a tradition as himself and might care to have this recognised. In the Venetian view there is nothing to encourage in Burano and, if there were, it should be content to sit receptively at the feet of Venice. Yet compared with Burano Venice has been a stagnant pool, culturally, for some time. Burano is full of cultural enthusiasms and good-will largely running to waste because it has no guidance and is given no sense of direction. What is needed is tactful support of the interesting and encouragement to improve well-meant but not very successful efforts. A person with the right approach is much more important than the amount of money spent. Too much guidance, the imposition of a point of view or a policy, could do more damage than the neglect which Burano has suffered during the long years of the extraordinary *fainéantisme* of the Venice City Authorities under a Christian Democrat majority. Now perhaps, there is a chink of light. The left wing alliance which now rules the city is, at present, much given to gestures of only doctrinaire significance such as parading cultural activities under the heading of whatever horror occupies the forefront of the official party mind. So, it arranged concerts under the banner of protest against the brutal oppressions in Chile. But this makes neither for a better concert, for more appreciation of the music or for a greater understanding of the Chilean situation. One hopes that such irrelevancies will drop away with the exercise of power. The most interesting political development for Burano is the proposed change in the composition of the Ward Councils. Till now the members have been chosen by the political parties in proportion to their voting strength on the City Council. In future members will be directly elected in each ward. As one Buranello mildly said:

The members of the Ward Councils chosen by the political parties are not always the best people for whatever activity is proposed. They are chosen chiefly to represent the point of view of their party, as good party men, and not because they are interested in getting things done. So many of them are rather useless and things get distorted and are done for the wrong reasons. If white says 'Yes', red is bound to say 'No' and vice versa and they never agree on anything and think only of their party's advantage. Most parties organise cultural and social activities of their own but these are chiefly to help their parties, not to make better conditions for people generally. They are not

48

interested in the activities of individuals but in increasing party membership.

This reflects also Burano's very moderate interest in politics, an attitude even more evident among the young people. Burano is one of those odd places found in most countries whose vote reflects the national average. In nearly every election since the war the Burano vote has coincided with the vote of Italy as a whole. By and large politics are regarded as the chosen preserve of those with axes to grind and the political parties as their tools. There is considerable resentment against mal-administration and particularly against the neglect of the interests and welfare of Burano but no great surprise that this should be so. There is also resentment about the present amount of unemployment. Most people believe that the government is the cause of the country's economic difficulties, not the victim, and are certainly not in a mood to give it credit for the economic miracle from which Burano has so signally benefited for the last fifteen years. The swing to the left in recent elections seems to be more an expression of dissatisfaction with the immobility of recent governments rather than a shift in political convictions. These four comments by separate speakers reflect the prevailing views:

—Burano is fairly interested in politics. We think politics are too much influenced by party considerations and by the desire to win tactical points. The stress is laid on things like the class struggle which does not mean anything to us in Burano. We are all the same here. So we think that the parties are not interested in constructing a better society but in scoring off one another. For ordinary people politics is a matter of voting against governments which do not know how to do their job. There is a lot of talk about reform and nothing ever gets done. There is no effective action in any field. Look at our old-fashioned methods, look at our justice and education. We need a moral clean-up in politics and administration. For instance if you declare your income honestly the Inspector of Taxes will not believe you and so you are forced, however unwillingly, into dishonesty. What is so strange is that all Italy must be thinking these things because, you know, Burano is a kind of political barometer. Our vote here nearly always reflects the national vote. This was so in the referendum on divorce, at the time of the constituent assembly after the war and in the referendum on the monarchy. Burano said 'Si, alla repubblica' and so did Italy.

—Italy has everything. We work hard, we are intelligent, inventive. We could be the richest country in Europe, richer than Germany, if we had a good government. What we need is honest men in the government and we need order, in our personal lives and our national life.

—No, no, no, no, we do not want the communists. People who vote communist do not know what they are doing. But we do need a proper government which knows how to act.

—Let those who want the communists go to Russia. I went to Moscow to have a look. Nothing to buy, nothing to eat. You can't say what you want. We can say anything we want. This is liberty.

There are, of course, small groups of enthusiasts for every party in Burano. The Communist Party has demonstrated its usual flair by managing to share the premises of the cinema and the Christian Democrats their usual ineptitude by having offices in a back street.

Religion, that other great formative influence on societies, excites as little interest as politics. To a few, and not only among the old, religious faith is still an important element in their lives. A few of the young go regularly to mass and take a serious interest in discussions on such subjects as the responsibilities of a Christian in the world of today. These discussions are led by a young priest who is much admired and respected and who cuts a wide swathe among the young people, providing them with opportunities to cut their teeth on quite tough theological and social subjects as well as helping them to organise *feste* and other jollifications. But, in general, some go to mass 'when they can', which is a

50

euphemism for very seldom, and most not all. Two women had this to say:

—The church counts less and less in our lives. Less and less.
—Yes, you get married in church, but now you don't even go the next Sunday, not even the women . . .
—But the women send the children. Oh, yes, every Sunday they go to mass. But themselves? Oh, no, never, not in Burano . . .
—Well, even the children go less often now, anyway the children of the younger women. And there is a good *parroco* (Parish priest) too . . .

What one might call the social element in religion is still important. Everyone, as far as I could discover, welcomes the priest each year to bless the house. Marriages are celebrated in church, the children are baptised and confirmed and the dead buried according to its rites. When faced with illness or pain, when in trouble, some still turn to the church, but rather than a religious impulse this is often a residual funk about hell.

As in most small, tight communities there is a strong sense of continuity with the dead. They were known and loved, or tolerated, as part of the community as well as of their families and this communal mourning is another example of Burano's impressive social cohesion.

The cemetery is a long way off in Mazzorbo over the wooden bridge which links it to Burano. Most funerals start from the parish church of S. Martino, cross the *piazza* and take the via Baldassare Galuppi, which is the main thoroughfare, shopping centre and strolling ground of Burano. It is normally a busy, bustling place but on certain days it has a feeling of subdued alertness about it, a quick look over the shoulder cast by the locals hanging around. Then there comes the sound of the ringing down of steel shutters over the shop fronts. Shopkeepers and customers line up outside, eyes reverently cast down as the funeral comes abreast, some making the sign of the cross with a muttered prayer as the coffin passes. The procession is headed by male relations and friends and representatives of the associations to which the deceased may have belonged, carrying wreaths, then comes the priest and then the coffin mounted on a light wheeled bier suitable for manoeuvring over bridges. The coffin is flanked by the pall-bearers who propel it. Then comes the family in order of precedence. Apart from the grief of the bereaved, the chief impression left with the outsider looking on is of the grave reverence of the Buranelli and the constant sound of shutters which clatter down as the funeral approaches and clatter up when it has passed and the shop re-opens for business and one feels the upsurge of that relentless cheerfulness of the Mediterranean which so thinly covers the substratum of melancholy of those same shores.

The cemetery in Mazzorbo is relatively new. It has not yet acquired much atmosphere of peacefulness and rest. The graves are always neat and sometimes lavishly decorated. As one Buranella said with a spice of malice:

> You see that it is not only in our houses that we are competitive. We must outdo the neighbours even when we put flowers on a grave of someone we loved. Just as we try to outdo them in furnishings, so when we die. In Burano we all want to be first. Oh, yes! We want to make a better showing with flowers than the other graves. We say that flowers are the last of life's garments. We have always spent a lot of money on flowers and nowadays we spend even more. We have got it to spend, now.

Since the population of Burano is Catholic in a careless kind of way it is subject to the proselytising attentions of sects such as Jehovah's Witnesses. These are viewed with silent and polite astonishment as another instance of the extraordinary dottiness to be found on the *terraferma*. It says much for the fervour of these sects that they continue to work such barren ground.

The third influence for order in society is the state, chiefly manifested in the police which, in Italy, is living through a particularly difficult period. In spite of the wave of violence they carry out their duty at the risk of their lives and during the last year a number have been killed by bank robbers and kidnappers. They are carefully selected from a large body of applicants, not very well paid, and their devotion to duty scarcely recognised. In the lagoon there is a good deal of

52

smuggling, as in any great port. Ships often lie outside Venice waiting for a tide, a pilot or the fog to lift. There is a constant legitimate traffic of fishing boats and in-shore craft which masks the activities of those carrying off contraband to quiet places in the lagoon and neighbouring *terraferma*. It falls to the Carabinieri and the Guardia di Finanza to check this. Apart from this the Buranelli do not have a good reputation in the eyes of their neighbours and, local chauvinism being what it universally is, the compliment is returned. There are people who will tell you that the Buranelli have two standards with regard to crime. There is thieving which is reprehensible because it is cheating and there is pinching which is acceptable (at a pinch) and is more allied to fiddling or to the late wartime concept of 'liberating' things. There is a good deal of thieving. Boats disappear (always to another island, if you believe what you hear), forays are made on the crops of neighbouring islands, particularly artichokes at the beginning of the season. Yet everybody leaves their washing to dry unattended in the *calle* and, so far at least, neither young nor old are ever molested. There was once a hold-up of a jeweller's shop when the thieves got away with a very good haul and the only casualty was a café waiter scared out of his wits by revolver shots.

There is also some illicit dealing in antiques in the lagoon. In Roman times it was used, as it still is, as a highway for trade and passengers and there must always have been depots and wrecked ships from which goods were lost. During the troubled period when the barbarian invasions caused so many hasty retreats to safety among tricky swamps, many household valuables must have been lost. They turn up from time to time and are too often not declared to the museum authorities as the law prescribes. There are also recurrent and unconfirmed rumours of sales of antiquities discreetly held in some remote part of the lagoon. One man told me:

My goodness, the things you find in the lagoon, beautiful little things. You find them chiefly over towards Altino where that Roman town was. There is nothing there now, just a few fields and a museum. Not very long ago the police were keeping a watch on one of the islands. They were selling antiquities out there. No, I don't know whether they caught them. I never heard. You know that drunkard we passed just now? He'll keep you talking all day about everything imaginable but you just say 'Antiquities' to him and he shuts up like an oyster and is off like a shot. Even when he is drunk he knows enough to shut up.

The police are among the few strangers working and living in Burano. Like them, the majority of the workers are now employed. The main change in Burano over the last two generations or so has been from a community of individuals engaged on their own account in traditional crafts to an employed society. This must in the long run involve a tremendous shift in attitudes. The present strength of Burano perhaps derives from the fact that the shift has not yet occurred, and that the characteristics developed by the old trades live on in a new context. One obvious distinction is that the old trades were, on the whole, lonely. A fisherman usually worked alone out in the lagoon in his little *sandalo*, the boatman delivering a load to another part of the lagoon was alone for most of the day. A woman applying herself to her day's stint of lace-making was likely to sit alone at her front door. If now lace-making has become an almost social occasion it is largely because it is no longer of any consequence economically. The solitary nature of much of their work must have been one of the factors which developed the self-reliance and independence which is such a marked characteristic of the Buranelli. It is perhaps a fallacy to think that it is the monotony of factory work which makes it so dreary, so soul-destroying. Yet nothing could be more repetitive than fishing or repeating the same stitch or the same stroke of the hoe thousands of times over. Possibly the danger to well-being lies more in the incompleteness of the job allotted to each worker and in the imposed rhythms, the regimentation which involve everyone making the same gestures at the same time. This kind of industrial monotony is seldom found in Italy where most industries are still small and artisan in character. The glass-blowing works in Murano are a case in point, since every object is hand-made. The

54

maestro or leader of a team and his assistants may not be solitary or have time to build up that rustic philosophy so much admired by romantic novelists, but each has his own specialist rôle in the skilled process of creating the finished object. To this extent there is an important difference between the employed worker in Burano and his brother in a thousand factories in the industrial world. He is still, in a sense, a producer, like the fisherman or the peasant, though he has, increasingly, protection against adversity afforded by employment (as against a day-to-day anxiety about providing for his family) and the membership of a trade union to support his expectations of continuing prosperity. He does not suffer from a feeling of frustration or the uselessness of ambition consquent on the industrial process. On the contrary, the employed worker in Burano feels that the future is his and his son is eager to follow in his footsteps. One hopes that they are right and that the prosperity of the last fifteen years will not turn out to be a lure to attitudes doomed to disappointment in a stagnating economy. It is the old trades which, at present, are breeding frustration: the fisherman who feels old-fashioned, almost redundant and certainly a failure by any economic yardstick unless he happens to have inherited good equipment and be blessed with enough brothers to run the boat among themselves, or the small shop-keeper battling with increasing competition and the complexities of new taxation.

Glass-blowing is an ancient and intricate trade and employment in it used to be confined almost entirely to the island of Murano because of distance and the difficulties of transport, even from Venice. Indeed, in order to preserve the valuable secrets of the materials and techniques used in the making of glass the Serenissima tended to confine the glass workers to the island of Murano, just as it exiled the furnaces there after a number of disastrous fires in Venice itself. The techniques used in the blowing of glass have scarcely changed since the earliest times. What have changed are the furnaces and the cooling ovens now fired by electricity and thermostatically controlled. This makes for higher production by greatly reducing waste and breakages. Until very recently glass-blowers learnt their trade by apprenticeship. Now there is a trade school in Murano which teaches the techniques but any *maestro vetraio* (master glass-blower) will tell you that it is still experience which counts. It takes twenty years, they say, to make a really fine master craftsman, and even then he is hard to find because he must also have imagination and be something of an artist. It must be said, too, that the craftsman in many factories now works to the specification of a designer which tends to reduce him from an artist to a technician and, to that extent, harms the tradition however lovely may be the objects produced. A small proportion both of the traditional and of the professionally designed production of Murano glass is still very lovely and now, necessarily, very expensive. Most of the objects produced are for the tourist trade. Unfortunately there is little attempt made to produce well-designed, small, low-cost objects to suit the pockets of the mass of tourists. Anything goes for them and the average seems steadily to decline and the shops are full of horrors, debased in taste and technique, which sell like hot-cakes to the uninformed tourist.

For the one master craftsman and his team of assistants a factory employs a large number of other tradesmen and many unskilled workers. Among these are many dead-end jobs. The girls wrap and pack the glass for sale in other cities and abroad. Their release from this boring occupation will come on marriage. The boys, mostly putting in time between leaving school and call-up for military service, push trolleys, lump parcels, run errands.

In quality and quantity of employment of Buranelli the glass factories come first and it is a relatively new trade encouraged by the great improvements made in the *vaporetto* transport services. There is a scattering of other jobs held by Buranelli which are more significant in providing variety of employment than for the number of livelihoods they offer the community. These run through most of the skilled trades, carpenters, masons, mechanics, secretaries, shop girls, to the run-of-the-mill labouring jobs. It is worth noting that Burano, that island of boatmen where you are practically born with an oar in your hand, now, for the first time in history, contributes gondoliers to Venice because they can travel between their station and their homes by *vaporetto*.

Of the traditional Burano-based trades the most important is still fishing. There is a little inshore fishing in the Adriatic from Burano. The boats used are usually the *bragoze* which originated in Chioggia and were adopted by the sea-going fisherman of the northern lagoon. These *bragoze* are, traditionally, gorgeously decorated on both hull and sails. When Queen Elizabeth II visited Venice in *Britannia* the fishermen of Chioggia sent their most beautiful boats sailing up to Venice to circle *Britannia* several times in a kind of royal salute. One of these *bragoze,* called *Afrodite,* and decorated with more than usual fantasy to match her name, is often to be seen in Burano although this is not her home port. She is usually moored near the *vaporetto* stop. These large boats require a crew of three or four men and are now extremely expensive to build and equip. They are mostly trawlers. Usually they are jointly owned by a family of brothers or cousins each of whom has a 'part' of the catch. These fishermen make a very reasonable living. Fishing within the lagoon is quite different. There the fisherman works alone or with one other, from a *sandalo*. This is a small, flat-bottomed boat with a little deck forward and a very low gunwale. In the old days it was rowed with two oars standing, facing the bows. This method of rowing they called *alla Valesana* or *alla Buranella*. In the fifties outboard motors became generally available and now almost every fisherman who reckons to make a living has one. Indeed this is the most important technical advance which has affected his trade, cutting down the time and hard work required in rowing to and from his fishing grounds and enabling him to get his catch to market quicker and fresher. The *sandalo* is a neat craft, swift, easy to manoeuvre and can penetrate into almost any narrow channel in the lagoon. In the old days they were always black, pitch being the best preservative, but since the introduction of oil paint they come in a variety of colours. Only the *gondola* and the *sandalo* plying for hire must, by ancient decree, always be black. The fishing is mostly done by dropping a net in a circle and scaring the fish into the mesh by whacking the surface of the water with an oar while rowing with the other, a tricky feat of balancing as well as oarsmanship. The net is then drawn in hand over hand and the fish tipped into the bottom of the boat to be transferred to a box kept in the cool under the decking. One of the pleasures of the lagoon at night is to watch the acetylene lights of the *sandali* weaving their way gently along the shallow edge of the *barene* and threading the little canals. This night fishing requires two men. One rows gently. The other stands poised in the bows just above the lamp with a trident in his hand ready to spear a sole or a quicksilver eel. For the latter he will use a narrow, three-pronged, barbed trident. For the flat fish, sole and flounders, he uses an eleven-pronged barbed trident. Both are made by a blacksmith living in Burano and are a perfect example of a tool as ancient almost as fishing itself, perfected through centuries of use and made today by the same method as when they were first used. Sometimes the fishermen when out after shellfish use a very long pole with a net fixed to a steel frame at the end. This they prod and drag across the floor of the lagoon and then, using the boat as a lever and their own weight in the boat as a counter-balance, heave it up to inspect their catch. This fishing is usually done alone and in the shallower parts of the lagoon. It is very heavy work.

A fisherman on the job is seldom idle. Now that he has an outboard motor he can prepare his nets and the other equipment on the way to the fishing grounds, steering the *sandalo* with an occasional nudge of elbow or knee. On the return journey he sorts and if necessary cleans his catch. It is a lonely trade and one which breeds independent decision and action. They do not talk much at any time or on any subject. So they do not talk much about freedom. It is doubtful whether they have formulated an idea of freedom with any clarity but this does not prevent a deep and passionate insistence on it as a way of life, which is very apparent in their actions and attitudes if not in their words. It is surprising that this independence, carried sometimes to the point of contrariness, should co-exist with a willingness to work together which the fishermen of Burano have so signally demonstrated in their co-operative. This ability to work together is in marked contrast to the attitude of the peasants in the neighbouring islands and *terraferma* who are so closed within their suspicion of other people's motives that they trust no one outside the strict limits of the family and not always then. Perhaps the fisherman's capacity to co-operate springs from the tolerance of the vagaries of others which is such a notable feature of the tight Burano community. Certainly there is no social stratification among them such as Peter Neile found in Apulia where the daughter of a cultivator of mussels could not aspire to marry the son of an oyster grower. The comment: 'There are no *signori* in Burano', applies to each part of the community as well as to the whole.

The other two trades connected with the lagoon are those of the boatmen and boat-builders. Freight of all kinds has always been carried about the lagoon in great wooden *topi* now equipped with powerful marine engines and, according to their size, capable of carrying anything from a houseful of furniture to an enormous weight of squared-off blocks of stone for rebuilding the great sea-walls, or *Murazzi*, which protect long stretches of the southern lagoon from the battery of Adriatic storms. There were, until quite recently, a number of boat-building yards and *squeri* for building and repairing smaller craft, mostly *sandali* and other boats used for fishing. Now there are very few left and the most interesting of them is Agostino Amadi's yard because a conscious and successful effort has been made to ally the old craftsmanship and quality with modern tools and equipment. The *mototopi* are usually manned by one boatman only and to watch the subtlety and precision of manoeuvre of these seemingly clumsy boats in narrow waters is a lesson in seamanship. Like the fisherman's, the boatman's is a solitary life, chugging about in all weathers in all parts of the lagoon. A few read newspapers and magazines standing astride the tiller and with an apparently idle but in fact very vigilant glance ahead, marking down the exact position and speed of every object in relation to themselves. Most watch the changing lagoon and in the course of many lonely hours come up with the same kind of reflective attitude of all who ply solitary trades whether boatmen or shepherds or foresters. Only one of them, as far as I know, is a musician and, being a shy man, only plays his trombone in the back stretches of the lagoon to the passing moorhens and the now so rare fishing heron.

The only traditional trades open to the women of Burano were domestic work and lace-making. It was mostly the girls and unmarried women who hired themselves out as servants because continual child-bearing and household chores combined with distance from Venice kept the married woman tied to her home. Burano women have a great reputation for cleanliness and energy and Venetian housewives were always glad to employ them. Domestic servants everywhere seem to be overworked and underpaid and there are now very few representatives of the regiment of girls who kept Venetian houses sweet and clean. The other trade of lace-making is also a dying trade and even if the efforts to revive the lace-school are a success it is difficult to see how the craft can be made economically viable. Lace, like all handwork, is or should be expensive to make. In addition it is hardly suitable for clothes designed for modern living, and altar cloths, ecclesiastical and other ceremonial robes are required in insufficient quantity to support an industry. It is also difficult to keep in impeccable order particularly in a period when everyone uses textiles which are easy to maintain. For all these reasons one can only assume that the lace-makers now at work will be the last of their kind.

The only new Burano-based trade is tourism. At first

glance, particularly in the summer months, it seems the most important aspect of the island. The roar of the huge tourist launches is a leit-motif to life in Burano throughout the tourist season. Bars, cafés, restaurants, stalls selling lace, Murano glass, postcards, and tourist kickshaws of every conceivable kind sprout wherever the tourist may be expected to wander. The owners of these shops make a profit and many make a living. The owners of the launches and the tourist agencies certainly make money. Yet the life of Burano is remarkably little affected by the horde of strangers that spend half an hour or so strolling across the *piazza* and down the main thoroughfare. Life during the summer seems to go on at two levels which touch only fleetingly and at a few points, such as the *vaporetto* station or perhaps at the tobacconist buying cigarettes or a stamp. The bars and the shops used by the locals are different from those which attract the general run of tourists. Occasionally one or two will be found buying a slice of ham or some peaches or figs and then the Buranelli usually courteously stand back and stop their chatter to stare at these strange beings who have so far stepped out of their rôle as twenty-minute strollers from another world as to enter a shop used by housewives. Even the *calli* used are different and at the height of the season one can walk across Burano without seeing a single tourist. 'No,' said one Buranello, 'tourists do not count in our lives. They only count for the stall-holders and the bars.'

This is most clearly seen during the evening stroll when everyone, almost without exception, turns out to take the air. The men, back from work, fed, contented, washed, in clean shirts and with hair slicked down, stand about in groups or make their way from café to café and table to table where the old men sit chatting. Nothing ever seems to be drunk: no glasses, no bottles are visible and the owners do not seem to mind. There are other bars where the drinking is done and there is a healthy if not bibulous din, down at the end of a dusky room. Some of the men push prams, airing the baby with their young wives all neat in a newly-ironed dress. What a lot of bandy fishermen there are! One wonders what it can be about fishing that makes them so. Children dash about on little bicycles making figures of eight and

61

never seem to collide with people or career off into a canal. The children and the dogs with their muzzles dangling from their collars are the only ones to show any turn of speed. The grown-ups proceed like a slow tide coming in over the sands, each wave going a little further than the last and receding to give way to another. They talk, they stroll, they inspect the shops: shoes, a new display in a grocer's window, shoes, ah! plums are in, shoes, fishing equipment, shoes. How do the Italians manage to get through so many pairs of shoes? By the time of the evening stroll the great press of tourists has departed to the early dinners they seem to insist on in their hotels but there are enough of them left to demonstrate how utterly indifferent are the Buranelli to their presence. The wave of strollers parts to pass them without ceasing their talk or changing their pace and join again behind them like a little spent wave going round a rock on the beach. They are not of the community. Therefore they do not exist. One knows immediately when one is accepted into the community. I knew I had been admitted when, one day, in the butcher's which was crowded as usual, a fisherman's wife said to the butcher pointing at me: 'Serve this *signora* first. She has to catch the *vaporetto* to Torcello.' I had ceased to be a stranger. My affairs were their affairs and I had graduated.

The Buranelli are home-loving people: 'When I see my crooked *campanile*, I know I'm all right. I'm at home.' They emigrate unwillingly and mostly for one of two reasons. The first is to find work. The Veneto is not rich either agriculturally or industrially and cannot compare in range of jobs or rewards with Lombardy or the great industrial cities of northern Italy. Since the beginning of the 1950s, some half-million people have emigrated from the Veneto. But few of them came from these lagoon islands. This was partly because the glassworks of Murano and the increase of tourism in Venice and such resorts as Jesolo along the Adriatic coast absorbed the available work force. Earlier, more men left to seek work, but even then it was not because it was not possible to live in Burano or Torcello (fishermen and peasants can always just manage, if not more, since they produce food) but in the hope of bettering themselves. Today those very few who leave are mostly in the hotel trade who go, when young, to learn English, French and German and, when older, because they see opportunities in the great hotels of the capital cities of Europe or America or, even more alluring to any Venetian mind, the chance of a little restaurant of their own. One of them summed up emigration for reasons of work in these words:

Now few emigrate from these islands. Before the war when work was hard to get some went away. A brother of mine went to Argentina but now he has moved to Germany. I have a nephew too in America. Some leave to do seasonal work in Switzerland. Some left who could have stayed. They did not have to go because there was no job at all but because they thought they could do better. I have a cousin who went for this sort of reason and now he would rather be at home but he cannot come back because the fare costs too much. He has not done too well and he has a family. He was one who made a mistake in thinking that he could do better.

But if the Buranello has not yet been caught up in the universal drift to the large cities a certain number have been forced out because of the housing shortage. The population now stands at a little under six thousand which is a considerable reduction from the eight thousand or so before the war. Consequently the people who have homes, and who have mostly bought them since the war, have been able to make themselves reasonably comfortable since they have more room and rising wages paid for installing good sanitation and kitchen accommodation. It is the newly married who find it difficult to get a house, and it is these who are being forced to leave Burano.

There is now a small gleam of hope that Burano may benefit from the overall plan for the protection and development of Venice, of which Burano is, administratively speaking, a part. In general this plan has been ill-received as pedestrian in concept and as failing to meet either the social or the conservation needs of the city. In particular it has been forthrightly and radically attacked by an expert group of Italian and foreign town-planners which discussed it under the auspices of Unesco in June 1975. In this planning process

Burano found itself, as usual, at the tail-end of the queue, pushed aside because of the greater importance given to other parts of the Venetian problem. This greatly depressed the Buranelli and many rumours flew around including the tale that the authorities proposed to halve the population of the island, though how this could have been achieved in a community of house-owners it is difficult to see. These delays in planning Burano's future may yet work out to the island's advantage. Certainly the thought now being devoted to its needs is, at the level of the officials concerned with town-planning, imaginative and sympathetic and shows considerable respect and understanding of the community. Whether the proposals now being worked out will be carried through at the political level remains to be seen.

Essential to the plan is a sufficient development of Burano's traditional trades to provide all those who want to earn their living within the island and lagoon with an opportunity to do so. This will be very difficult to achieve because the traditional crafts (fishing, fish farming in the *valli*, boat-building, lace-making), are no longer attractive economically or in meeting new career or status expectations. In addition many aspects of this development such as distribution, marketing and the division of profits would require some protection of local industries which would probably require national legislation which, in Italy, is always slow and chancy.

The proposals for housing are likely to be of more immediate interest to the Buranelli, who seem, in any case, to be quite happy with their recently-found employment in Murano and further afield. Indeed their commuting time (though considered appalling by Venetians who reckon to walk to their work in twenty minutes) compares well with that in most of the large cities of Europe. The only place where extra housing could be located is in the neighbouring island of Mazzorbo which is joined to Burano by a wooden footbridge. The proposal is to build there a new village on the traditional Burano lines of small one-family houses preserving all the attractions of the old settlement while providing more space and modern plumbing. This new village is being planned as a separate but contiguous community with its own shops, school, church and so on.

This seems an enlightened proposal and is likely to appeal to the Buranelli particularly if the idea of a public meeting to discuss the plan with them is carried out. A meeting of this kind, skilfully handled, would give the Buranelli, for the first time in their history, an opportunity to comment on their future and the feeling that they counted and could exert some influence on the material conditions of the community in which they live. This form of consultation, combined with the new arrangements likely to be adopted for electing individuals to the Ward Councils instead of the political parties nominating members according to their voting proportions in the City Council, would be a huge step forward. It would give a great impetus to local initiative and remove many of the frustrations from which the community suffers. It is so much to be hoped that the politicians give effect to these enlightened proposals.

A Boat Builder

Boat-building is one of the traditional crafts of Burano and Agostino Amadi one of its most up-to-date exponents. In his big hangar the prevailing atmosphere is one of orderly and cheerful business. Whether he is there or whether he isn't the work proceeds at that unhurried craftsman's pace which ensures quality work completed on time. There is of course some mess from the day's work, heaps of shavings, odd-ments of wood and rejected bits and pieces but no old litter in corners or old paint pots left around. Tools taken from the racks are put back in their proper places when done with — order so that work can be done properly, not tidiness for tidiness' sake. Through the wide doors at the end of the hangar the slip is equally orderly and if you raise your eyes you see, across the water and the *barene*, the basilica of Torcello flanked by its *campanile* and Santa Fosca with its Byzantine domes squatting on its other side. It can't be often that a boat-building yard has such a view.

Agostino Amadi fits the place: late thirties, slim, in-telligent, straightforward, decided, courteous, hard-working with a small shy smile, to call him dedicated would be to make him too intense. But here is a man who cares, for his

65

craft and for the quality of the boats he makes.

'We Amadis have been boat-builders here in Burano for generations. The first one we know about is my great-grand-father Agostino, then my grandfather Achille, my father Giovanni and myself another Agostino. The name Agostino Amadi painted up outside the yard is me. We change the name with each generation. My father and his brother Antonio inherited jointly but decided to split the business and since then there have been two Amadi boat-building yards next door to one another. Both are now run by their sons, that is to say with my cousins on one side and me on the other. One of my brothers has a yard here in Burano and does a similar business to mine. My other brother has a yard in Mestre but he has developed his business rather differently and is mostly concerned with storing motor launches and sailing boats through the winter though he does some repairs as well. These brothers are much older than me and set up their businesses while my father was still active.

I had the usual amount of schooling here in Burano and then came into the yard. I came in straight from school without any technical or theoretical training. We have always been craftsmen, artisans in my family and our skills have been handed down from father to son. My father taught me and I learn every day from doing the job. I don't think it would have helped me to have had a technical training. By the time I was eighteen I was beginning to get ideas about modernising the boatyard and equipping ourselves with up-to-date tools to help us in our work. I must have been a trial to the old man, badgering and criticising all the time. Finally he said, 'All right, you do it your way. You be in charge for a year and then we will see.' I don't know what he thought the result would be. At any rate at the end of the year (I was nineteen by then) he let me go on and here I still am. That was eighteen years ago.

Over the years we have rebuilt and re-equipped the place. When I took over it was really a little old *squero* (a little yard for repairing small craft) with a rickety sort of lean-to and piles of wood stacked about the place without rhyme or reason. Now, as you can see, we have got it fairly convenient. In this big hangar we can build two *mototopi* at a time and a number of smaller craft, and there is a smaller shop on the other side of the *calle* where we can build *sandali* and such like. We have electric saws and power hand tools in racks convenient to the working places. The wood, all sawn and sorted according to use, is stacked in racks along the walls and slung in cradles between the pillars and upstairs we have another big wood store. Outside on the slip we now have an electric crane.

The work we do in this yard is done just as it was two hundred years ago. We are helped by all this modern equipment but the methods and results are exactly what they were then only the work is more perfected, more exact thanks to precision tools. We no longer have to use an adze to fine down a plank. We use an electric saw and get a more exact fit — and so a better boat — but the boat is basically the same boat produced by the skill of a craftsman. If we want to give a curve to a plank we use the old method of alternate application of fire and water just as they did 200 years ago. And like then we still use good, solid, suitably seasoned wood. We never use these compressed or synthetic wood substitutes.

I work on every job if I possibly can but I get called away pretty often visiting clients, getting orders, smoothing difficulties. I have a fast, light boat and can usually tie up at the offices I have to go to but we are beginning to have a parking problem in Venice, too. This powerful little boat is invaluable because I simply do not have time to take the *vaporetto*. The *vaporetto* service is excellent and constantly improving but I can't afford the time it takes. Thirty minutes to the Fondamenta Nuove and then fifteen to twenty minutes on my feet to my appointment. When I am wanted back here! No, not possible! Then after all this running about and keeping things going in the yard and doing jobs myself I have this wretched paperwork to do when the men have gone and it is a bit quieter. I am usually here till half-past seven or eight in the evening, having started at seven in the morning. So far, it is all right (I am not yet forty) but I do sometimes wonder what is going to happen later. We don't know what happened before my great-grandfather's day because in a craft business like ours they did not keep records and contracts in those days. I wish I did not have to. My wife helps me in the office and does all our typing.

Although we are well-equipped we are still artisans and we all work together. This, I think, is important. At present, working with me I have three specialist craftsmen and four apprentices. One of the things which really worries me is the replacement of skilled craftsmen. It is very difficult to get young men interested. They don't want to do this sort of work any more. It is hard, heavy work. I need an intelligent, alert lad, ready to take responsibility and finding satisfaction in his work. Nowadays everybody is on the lookout for secure white-collar jobs in government or municipal service. I recently lost a very good craftsman to a job of this kind. He was really skilled and gifted too and had a real *colpo d'occhio*, a quick judgment and appreciation of a problem and the best solution. It wasn't a matter of pay, it was the life he did not want. The skilled craftsman is disappearing and, I am afraid, a lot of trades will disappear with him.

Our speciality these days is building big transport boats for goods of all kinds — chiefly *mototopi*. At one time we also built *peatole* and *corline, batteli* and *sandoli*, all of them rowing boats. Now we have restricted our range because of motorisation. The boat which has proved to be best adapted for use with an engine is, without doubt, the *mototopo* which is the usual transport boat which you see in Venice and, for this reason, it is the one used by all the big transport firms. Eighty per cent of our work is building these boats, the rest is mostly building a similar kind of boat for use in the port of Venice. These are smaller craft such as *topetti, sandali, coffani, san pierotte*. These are also sometimes used as pleasure boats. For general transport, besides the *mototopi* we are building a few *corine, marare* and small Burano fishing boats, which are intended chiefly for use in the lagoon but which can go out to sea, in favourable weather. These are a modified version of the *mototopo* but have a wider hull and some other features which make it more seaworthy for work in the open sea.

We design all the boats. By this I mean that we build them on the basis of our experience and practical knowledge. I do what designing seems necessary but, in fact, we depend on experience. We build a great many boats and we make modifications here and there, perfecting our methods all the time. In fact designs are very seldom useful to us in building a boat. We make one chiefly for the clients' satisfaction and not for our own use except as a rough and ready guide to measurements. We depend on our experience though of course always carrying out the clients' instructions and incorporating what we have learnt from the last job, correcting any errors and generally trying to perfect our practice. And so, bit by bit, we alter our methods.

Usually the way I work, and I think this is very important, is to give my men the outline, the profile if you like, of the hull, the *scomparto* we call it. In fact it is a sketch of the framework of the boat with an indication of measurements. If I have time I like to choose and cut the wood myself. If I do not have the time I entrust the work to one of the skilled craftsmen who, I know, is able to judge which cuts of wood are best adapted for one part of the work or another.

We use oak exclusively for the framework of a boat and also for the hull because oak is much the most solid, compact, resistant wood and very long-lasting. Then there is larch which we also use a good deal. Pine we only use for secondary work, for example for the *paiolato* (flooring) and other moveable parts of the boat because they must be light to be easily shifted about. But for the hull and the body of the boat that have to stand up to wear we use oak and larch and elm, which is rather more flexible. We mostly get these woods from Europe. Fifteen or twenty years ago we used to use only Italian woods. We could still get enough of the quality we needed. Now we mostly get the oak we need from France, Czechoslovakia or Russia. Naturally I do not import wood myself. I do not use enough to make it worth while. I get it from a timber yard. I choose the trunks myself and get the timber-yard to saw them into planks to my specifications of thickness, taking into account the shape and diameter of the trunk and the use I intend to make of it. No tree-trunk is quite straight. In fact it would be a nuisance to me if it was as I should have to bend it to suit my needs. My job is to judge the best use I can make of the natural curve of the trunk I have selected to fit the construction of a boat. You learn to judge all this by experience and when I select a tree-trunk at the timber-yard I already see in my mind's eye just where I shall use it in building a boat.

There are certain curves in the framework of a boat that you cannot hope to get from the natural curve of a tree-trunk. To get the curve we want we still use the old method of applying heat and water alternately. First we heat the wood, then we soak it, forcing it gradually into the shape we want. Fire, water, fire, water. It takes time but bit by bit we make it go the way we want it.

It is difficult to say how long a *mototopo* takes to build because we make them of so many different sizes, with different characteristics and finishes. The classic *mototopo* of the simplest style without refinements but very robust and of medium size, that is to say with a carrying capacity of about 60 tons and measuring 12 metres by 2.60 metres would probably take two men forty to fifty days' work. This is only a rough estimate because we don't work in fixed teams but according to the needs of the job. So sometimes you will see one man working alone, sometimes three or four, and everybody in the yard may be called on to help with certain jobs. But say forty to fifty days to complete the boat. In addition we have to install the motor unless the client has made other arrangements. But we usually reckon to do it, and then when the client takes delivery he takes the boat over with the keys in his hand as we say.

Many boat-owners, particularly fishermen, become very proud of their boats and decorate them beautifully. They are particularly fond of angels and names embellished with arabesques. Sometimes they just ask for a particularly good paint job with gay colours and this also has the advantage of protecting the wood. The big transport firms don't usually pay much attention to ornamenting their boats. They just paint them in their house colours. But the private owner wants to give his boat an individual look like his house or his clothes. The *bragoza* fishing boat is particularly suitable for decorating. It was originally a Chioggia boat and the fishermen down there still decorate and maintain them most lavishly. They are charming boats from the aesthetic point of view. They are so appealing that we are asked to build them as pleasure boats, adapted for living in with a cabin in the prow to sleep two or three, a galley, shower, sail locker and so on, in such a way as to retain the characteristic external appearance. These are sometimes very beautifully decorated by quite well-known painters. The fishermen, particularly, often like their decorations to have some meaning to them. They usually represent their patron saint. Swordfish and octopus are very popular and so are seabirds. We have boys here in the yard who enjoy doing these designs and are quite gifted and they sometimes do a private deal with the owner for decorations. There are also painters who specialise in boat ornament.

As I was saying earlier, we now only build types of boats that are well adapted to the marine engine. There were many types in use twenty or thirty years ago which we never build today, such as the *battelo cuor di gambero* which was a largish, working boat looking rather like a gondola. It had a raised poop but the prow was different and it was not built on a curve like the gondola. Builders in Venice used to use it for transporting sand and other building materials. The point of it was that it responded beautifully to the oar — again like a gondola.

Business has not been very good during the last year or

two. We have had fewer orders for boats; the price has increased enormously owing to the high cost of wages and materials, wood, nails, and particularly things like steel which has to be specially hand-forged for each boat. Some costs have increased six-fold in the last two years. Tools which we use every day and of course have to replace from time to time. I took out some tools which I had bought two years ago and saw they were still wearing their price tags. They were a third of the price they are asking now in the shops.

On the other hand I cannot see that any boat could serve local Venetian conditions better than the *mototopo*. Nowadays they are making boats of all kinds of materials, of plastic and iron and even concrete. I don't see how any of these materials could stand up to Venetian conditions, particularly the *moto ondoso* (the wash created by fast-moving motor boats in enclosed waters). Just think how boats are bashed about on the Grand Canal. They are continually bashed about from all directions, bash, bash, bash. Any rigid material like iron or concrete is bound to suffer and to make plastic sufficiently robust would be very expensive.

Our *mototopi*, precision-built of good woods by expert craftsmen, if they are properly and regularly maintained last up to thirty or even forty years. The other day I had a *peata* in for maintenance which my father made thirty-eight years ago. Imagine, it was built before I was born. And the construction was exactly what I would do myself today if I were building a *peata*. It is an old boat now, of course, but it can still carry its maximum load of about 34 tons. It is used as a lighter (it has no engine) and every morning takes on a load which usually averages 15 to 20 tons from a ship and is towed off by a *mototopo* or a little tug along with other lighters and *peate* to unload at the Tronchetto or at warehouses along the Scomenzera Canal.

To last as long as this boats must be regularly maintained and these working boats do not always get the care they should. A boat should really be checked twice a year. A small check-up in the spring say and a major check-up in the autumn or vice versa. By maintenance I mean hauling it out of the water, cleaning the hull, particularly the underwater

72

parts, checking the wood and ironwork, scraping and renewing the paint where necessary, generally going over the whole structure to see that everything is in order, and refloating the boat. It is not generally recognised that when a boat is not working but lying idle in the water it deteriorates much faster than when it is working its way through the waves. So regular overhauls are even more important. But if a boat is lucky and gets regular attention it should have a useful life of at least thirty years. I am talking about boats. Marine engines are different. They have to drive a boat constantly against the pressure of the water and so are under the same sort of strain as a lorry engine going up a hill. You can judge the pressure of the water by the fact that if you shut the engine off the boat soon drifts to a standstill. A boat doesn't need brakes like a lorry. The water acts as a brake. Of course if you need to stop quickly you bang it into reverse.

Because of the shortage of orders I looked round for other work and put in a tender to build a *pontile* (a pontoon landing-stage) for A.C.N.I.L. (the Venetian municipal *vaporetto* service). I won the tender but had a little trouble actually getting the order because I had never built a *pontile* before. So I went and complained and got the order. When I got home I said to myself: "Right, now you've got a problem. What are you going to do? Where are you going to start?" You see these *pontili* are heavy, solid structures and the usual way was to work from underneath building the base. Imagine driving in all those nails above your head where you have no purchase on the thing. Not on your life. So I decided to reverse the procedure and build the base upside down as though it were a deck. That was quite easy as we were hammering in the nails with a normal downward stroke. Then — and I was a bit worried about this in case I had miscalculated — we towed the base down the slip with two *mototopi* with the tow-ropes lashed to the two landward corners. What I was reckoning on was that, given the buoyancy of the water, it should be quite easy to turn the platform over. And so, after a sickening moment, it happened. Then we hauled the platform back up the slip and built the rest of the *pontile* on top of it which was quite easy as we were hammering downwards with a normal stroke. So

73

it proved to be an easy job and I hope to make some more. But, would you believe it, none of the firms who made *pontili* had ever thought of doing just that? And now they all do it, if you please!'

Two Fishermen

The first fisherman who talked to me was a man of the old school. Angelo Trevisan, *cavaliere ufficiale* of the Order of Vittorio Veneto, has an excellent record in two wars and has devoted thrity years of his life to organising the fishermen's co-operative in Burano which has done much to improve the technical competence and consequently the earning capacity of his fellow-fishermen in the island. He is now eighty-nine and actively engaged in enjoying the considerable fruits of his toil, skill and thrift in a trade which he entered eighty-two years ago.

'The first time I went fishing I was seven years old. I hid one night in my papa's boat and he only found me when we were already on our way. He wanted to turn back to take me home but my uncle (because these two brothers always fished together) said, No, we don't have time to go back, we will miss the tide. It won't hurt the lad to stay with us for once. So we went on. I was so full of enthusiasm, so delighted to be going fishing at last that I did not sleep a wink. My father and uncle began to fish *a palpone*. At low tide just when the water runs out of the *ghebi* (shallow canals) you can pick up fish, like that, with your bare hands, without nets or anything. You can pick up ten or twenty kilos of fish if you know where to go. You pick them up quick, bang, bang, bang into the bottom of the boat with the greatest of ease. Then, very early the next morning, the various *sandoli* which had been fishing in this way in the *ghebi* all assembled and we went off together to sell the fish. That first time my enthusiasm went to my head and my father kept my catch apart from the rest and I sold it for 45 cents. At that time a man was satisfied with his night's fishing if he made a catch worth two lire as you can imagine how proud I was that a little boy like me had caught 45 cents' worth on his first try. I was taught to fish by good fishermen who reckoned to get five, six, eight or ten lire a night.

Now I will tell you about fishing for *novelami*. These are tiny fish, tiny, newborn fish, like fine little hairs. Every year the *Capitaneria* of the Port of Venice fixes the season for taking *novelami*. When the season comes round the

fishermen approaches the owners of the *valli* to see what kind of fish they want. They usually want *cefali* (grey mullet), *orate* (bream) and *branzini* (sea bass) when they could get it. Then we would arrange to fish them and sow these little articles in their enclosures or fish farms. At the same period you could fish mature fish. What you went after depended on what sort of nets and equipment you had. But we went after *novelami*. Even if the *Capitaneria* had allowed you to fish them beyond the season they fixed you could not have done it with the equipment for fishing *novelami*, because as the fish grew they became wily and sometimes quite fierce and would defend themselves and tear the nets. Young *cefali*, in particular, leap about and drive through the net. They are not passive fish like sole or *passerini* (a small kind of flounder) which lie quietly on the bottom doing nothing. You just scoop them up. But *cefali* and the others you had to fish by other methods suitable for taking agile, adult fish.

Generally speaking the *Capitaneria* allows fishing for periods of a hundred days for the various kinds of fish. You have to be able to resist temptation because you get into trouble if you fish outside the fixed period. In the spring the special thing is the *novelami*, but of course there are all the other fish as well. In the autumn there are the *granchi* (shore crabs) which, when they moult and discard their old shells, become what we call *moleche*. Very delicate, very tasty, are *moleche*. At this time we also fish *mazenetto* (red mullet), *schile* also called *cannochie* (mantis shrimps) and *gamberini* (prawns) and all the other articles.

In the spring the fish come into the lagoon from the sea and when it starts to get warm they go into the canals and the *ghebi* to feed and that is where we mostly fish them. There they stay from about the second half of June, the whole of July and August and also in September. When it gets really cold the fish which cannot stand the low temperatures in the shallow waters of the lagoon leave their pastures and go back to the sea to save their lives. They go right down through the Adriatic and across the Mediterranean. The reason is that in the Adriatic we have *secchi* (periodic oscillation of the sea level) and many parts of that sea become shallow and cold and to save themselves from the rigours of winter the fish have to find deep water, really deep water. Even the *passerini* and the *sogliole* (sole) migrate in this way as we fishermen have known for a very long time.

The fish know, just as we do, when the spring comes and they come up from the sea to their pastures in the lagoon, full of hunger, full of the desire to eat after the winter. You see them all swarming in: *passerini*, *sogliole* (sole), *cefali*, *anquille* (eels) and some *branzini* too, but not so many because they are not very fertile and in any case prefer the sea, as do the *orate*. Both of these become very cunning and know how to look out for themselves. The *cefali* come and go, come and go between the lagoon and the sea but seem to prefer the lagoon, like the *seppie* (cuttlefish), *passerini* and the little soles. So the fishermen prepare the proper equipment for the particular fish they want to go after.

The fish that best stands up to warmth is the eel because it tucks itself into the mud. If it does not it gets a sickness and develops red spots on its skin and dies. But the minute it gets a little bit cooler at night or after a storm, it comes out of its hole in the mud, has a good feed and hides again in the bottom of the canals in the lagoons. So the fisherman has to seize his moment for catching them. You mostly fish eel at night, particularly if there is a moon. In the day-time you have to look for their holes. If you have enough experience you can plot the holes here and there. There are usually three holes. The fisherman, in his *sandaletto* which can negotiate canals with very shallow water, looks for the hole where the silt is least disturbed and where there is the track of an eel going directly to the hole. Then he takes his *forcina* (a long-handled fork with very sharp barbed prongs) and plunges it in beyond the track. If he has judged right the eel immediately thrashes about and puffs up a little cloud of silt. Then the fisherman pulls up the *forcina* very slowly because he can't see yet whether he has the eel securely impaled on the barbs, and he brings it on board. You can catch five or six kilos of eel on a good night. Not always of course. If he got that every night the fisherman would soon be a multi-millionaire.

When I was a child the nets and other equipment cost very little. The trouble with the nets was that they were made of cotton and tended to rot and not stand up to wear and tear in seawater. About twice a month we had to soak them in a dye made of ground pine bark. This stiffened the nets and strengthened them for a while but you had to repeat this treatment frequently to prevent them rotting.

There are very sudden storms in the lagoon but you can see them coming and we have a good deal of experience of them. When you see one blowing up you make for the nearest *barena* and moor the *sandalo* and sit it out. Summer.

77

storms do not last long, half an hour perhaps, and the sun comes out again. Winter storms are different but then we do not fish much in the winter. In the first place there are very few fish, as we have said most of the fish migrate. Then your nets and other equipment are in a poor state of repair after a busy autumn's fishing and if you tried fishing with them you would lose most of your catch. So you spend the winter overhauling your boat and putting to rights your nets and equipment.

You know, there are some who are good fishermen and some who are not so good and in this trade you earn according to your skill. Now, I was a good fisherman, very skilful, really skilful and I have put most of my earnings into property. I have in my lifetime bought a lot of property, all earned by my fishing. But then I have never sold my catch to a wholesaler. I had a stall in Murano. Me, a Buranello, had a stall in Murano and I was very well known there. Just think, I first saw that stall at about the age of five and a half or six years old when I first went to it with my grandfather: I did not sell fish when I was so little but I used to take the heads and trimmings of the fish from the stall and the small fish I caught myself round to the houses for the cats and each of my customers used to give me something, ten or fifteen cents.

I learnt to fish by watching my father and uncle and by working out why they did the things the way they did. And then I was not content any longer with catching little fish in a childish way and I used to say to them: "You take a rest and let me do it", and very soon I was taking more fish than they were. And my father used to grumble: "You'll be a ruddy millionaire, you will." And I must say I am very comfortable. I do not mean to boast, in fact I am not boasting but I have a number of houses and agricultural land and shops which I let; we'll live very well on the rents, my daughter and I, and there will be plenty for her when I am gone. I have one bit of land on the *terraferma* which brings in a good rent and, in addition, enough grapes to make about 350 litres of wine every year. Good red wine. That is what I call good business. I helped to start the fishermen's co-operative here in Burano and I ran it for thirty years and never took a sou for doing it. I have always had money coming in from my fishing and I did not want to take money out of the co-operative. I used, of course, to take the expenses we all got for attending council meetings but we always drank that up waiting for the *vaporetto.*

Young men are still going into fishing, especially if their families have a boat and equipment. A family with reasonable skills and good equipment and which sells its catch at the fish market at the Tronchetto in Venice can earn a million lire a week during the fishing seasons. Young men can join the fishermen's co-operative at the age of eighteen. But the trouble is that people throw their money around these days, spending it on food and drink and their friends and going to the barber's shop to be made pretty. It is like those others, the more they study the more cretinous they become. Wherever the devil is, there is always abundance, as they say. If you know your job you can make a good living out of fishing. I have always fished alone, just me in my *sandalo.* I know fishermen mostly work in pairs but I've never seen the sense in it. There is always one who does all the work and the other who sits and watches him do it — and then they divide the takings. I ask you, where is the sense in that for the one who has done the work?

But if you are going to make a decent living and put something by you must know your job. It is particularly important to know the tides and the lagoon. You know the tides depend on the lunar cycle. Every fifteen days the tides swing from the *ponto* to the *acqua morta* and back again. At the time of the *acqua morta* or dead water there is very little movement of the water. The movement is greatest at the period of the *ponto.* At the time of *acqua morta* the outgoing tide, which we call the *dozana,* moves more slowly than the incoming tide or *savente,* and that is why *acqua alta* in Venice always happens at the time of the *acqua morta* because the old tide has not had time to get out of the lagoon before the next tide starts coming in. We say:

Sete, oto, nove, l'acqua non se muove.
Vinti, vintiun e vintido l'acqua no va ne su ne zo.*

*On the seventh, eighth and ninth (day after the new moon) the water does not move. On the twentieth, twenty-first and twenty-second (after the new moon) it goes neither up nor down.

We also say: *"Acqua morta è pesce morto"* (at the *acqua morta* the fish is dead). It is very little use going fishing then. The man who knows his tides and the movements of the waters and who is a competent fisherman will bring in a catch of fifty kilos when an incompetent fellow will bring in ten kilos.

Now all fishermen have outboard motors of five, ten, twenty, forty horsepower depending on the weight of their boats. So many horses in the lagoon and I never had one! All my life I rowed my *sandalo*. But then I am eighty-nine years old and all these new-fangled things only came in, in the sixties. After my time!

I have served in two wars. Eleven years in all counting my military service. In the Libyan war of 1911-1912 I was at sea nearly all the time but in the war of 1915-1918 I was in Venice for the whole war. I had got crafty by then! Of course, I think I was useful in my shore job. In any case I ended up in charge of my outfit. I was not called up in the last war but by then I was fifty-four.'

*

The second fisherman was a much younger, less skilful, less happy man. He was aged about forty and was sitting on the gunwale of his boat moored at the quay outside his house. Propped across the boat was a broad sloping board with a sack of crabs at one end of it and beside him at the bottom of the boat a plastic tub. He was quite pleased to have a companion and to chat, though without ever raising his eyes from his task.

He shook out a mass of angry, struggling shore crabs from the sack and with extraordinary quick deft movements picked out the females to throw into the tub, pushing the males aside into heaps which he swept from time to time into the canal.

'It is the season of *moleche* now. I went out earlier this morning to raise the nets and, as you see, I have caught a nice lot. If I fill this tub, and I think I shall, I can count on having 50 kilos to sell.

In the old days it would have taken me all the morning to

80

row out to the nets, put the catch into sacks and row back. This morning it took me about forty minutes with this out-board engine. It is rather expensive to run — it is a twenty horsepower engine — but I need some power because the boat as you can see is heavy and square-built. It is not the sort of boat we build here but it is sturdy and does my work very well.

What takes the time with *moleche* is the sorting. Only the females are good to eat and I have to work fast to get them into the tub and covered up with wet sacking in the cool as soon as possible so that they remain in good condition until the wholesaler takes them over. Also I want to get rid of these bad-tempered male crabs as soon as I can. You have to watch your fingers and your toes. Look at them, snap, snap, snap! They nip you as soon as look at you. They don't do any harm in the canal here. They scuttle off as fast as they can and, in any case, the next tide will carry them back into the lagoon.

I sell my catches to the wholesalers. I do not find it practical to sell privately. For one thing I should have to go to Venice and back and that would be half a day wasted and maybe missing a tide as well as the expense of fuel for the engine. And then I am liable to have the catch left on my hands and fish is very perishable. These *moleche* for instance are almost a luxury. Not everybody eats them every day and I could not be sure of selling a whole tubful myself. So I accept the wholesaler's offer. For this lot I expect I shall get 700 lire a kilo. The wholesaler will sell them for 1,400 lire a kilo. I think it would be fairer if I got more than half the final price. I've done all the work. He just makes a few telephone calls. The government should do something about all these middlemen, but have you ever heard of our government doing anything — except for themselves, of course?'

Two Glass-workers

The prosperity of Murano and Burano has gone hand in hand over the past generation. As the ancient craft of glass-making expanded in Murano to meet the demands of new markets it found a convenient supply of manpower in

Burano. The Buranelli, for their part, seeking a way out of the unprofitable round of traditional livelihoods, were eager to accept stable and relatively prosperous jobs. With their background of craft skills and independence of spirit the Buranelli fitted well into the almost medieval guild attitudes of glass-blowing. So both sides profited and the movement towards jobs in Murano was accelerated by improvements in the *vaporetto* services between the islands. This eliminated the long, cold, tedious journey by rowing-boat endured by an earlier generation of Burano glass-workers. Now the Murano glass-works provide the people of Burano with more jobs than any other trade.

Two glass-workers talked about their trade.

The first was Alberto Torcellan, a *maestro*, a master glass-blower. He lives in a little house not far from the church. One is welcomed straight into the kitchen which has a perfection of cleanliness and order found in a well-run ship. One wall has been cut away to form a broad arch into the sitting-room and here stand some fine examples of the *maestro's* skill. Particularly beautiful is a fifteen-inch-high goblet, elegantly engraved. It is flanked by a set of wine glasses of a purity of line and brilliance of crystal which embody the best tradition of Venetian glass, a tradition so dishonoured by the technically admirable but aesthetically dreadful run-of-the-mill tourist production of most Murano glass-works. Alberto Torcellan is an artist. He has the artist's capacity to manipulate materials into beautiful forms. Outside his craft his passion is music and he is the conductor of a little orchestra on the island. This is what he had to say about his craft:

'Few glass-blowers know the history of glass-making, which is a pity because it is a craft with a long tradition and we in Murano make it just as it has always been made. People know that it dates back to the time of the Phoenicians and that sort of thing, and that is about all.

Glass is a fusion of minerals and is made on the basis of sand, soda, nitrates, potassium and many others. The sand here in the lagoon is no use for making glass. We import the sand we use from France. It comes from the forest of Fontainebleau. Many years ago the sand used to come from

Pola on the Istrian peninsula, where most of the stone used in building Venice came from, and which is now in Yugoslavia. But that sand did not give a really pure crystal. It had green lights in it which is usually an indication of too much iron in the sand. We find the sand from Fontainebleau gives a perfect glass and this is because of the balance of minerals it contains.

I have worked for twenty-nine years in the same glass-factory, very nearly all my working life. The methods of work have not changed in my time and have probably not changed for hundreds of years. I am talking about the actual blowing of the piece. Of course we have up-to-date electrical furnaces and all that sort of thing but the actual making of the piece is still done by methods worked out centuries ago.

In my factory we make everything by hand. Every single piece which leaves the factory has been hand-blown by a master craftsman. There are almost no factories in Murano which make machine-made glass. Moulded glass and so on is right outside the tradition of Murano glass manufacture. Murano glass is blown glass and nothing else.

What has changed in my twenty-nine years is the *maestranze* (the master craftsmen). All those I knew when I was a lad and who taught me my trade are dead or very old now. A *maestro* is a master-craftsman who knows every-thing about the craft and which he has perfected by long experience. It usually takes eighteen to twenty years to become a *maestro*. I have known men start working as *maestri* after sixteen years or so but to reach full maturity and mastery of the techniques, to know *how* to work and to have gained full command of all aspects of the art, I think you need twenty years. And even then you go on learning. There is never an end to learning. You learn by time and ex-perience. The gifts a *maestro* chiefly needs are skill, I mean deftness with your hands, some intelligence and imagination. Without imagination a man cannot hope to become a *maestro*. In fact, if you don't have something of each of these attributes it is not much use trying to learn the trade. You do see boys of seventeen or eighteen who are already *maestrini* and you can pick out immediately, at a glance, those we call the *negati* (unfit) who just do not have what it takes to become a good *maestro*. They may develop into valuable assistants but they will never make a *maestro*. He has to have certain gifts just as a painter does. I do not have those gifts or skills. I am just a little bit of a musician but I would never make a painter.

A *maestro* cannot work alone. He must be helped and helped skilfully by people who understand the craft and who know what the next step will be and who hand him the right tools at the right moment and generally give alert assistance. They are mostly boys and we are in rather a difficulty about them at the moment because the compulsory school age has recently been raised to sixteen. Now at sixteen boys don't want to go into a glass-works to learn the trade, not because they would not be properly paid, because they would be nowadays, but because they know that the art of glass-blowing has to be learnt young and that sixteen is too old. The second reason is that is it a heavy trade, not in the way that a labourer's job is heavy but because you are always working in the heat of a furnace. For this reason, *maestri* are very often neurotic, bundles of nerves. A *maestro*'s job is very demanding. He has to be constantly on the alert, noticing and controlling every little thing because, unless everything has gone exactly as it should, his finished piece will shatter, will shiver into little bits when it is put into the *tempera* (cooling oven). Every piece of glass has to be tempered. It has to go into the *tempera* heated to a point equivalent to that of the piece and the heat is gradually reduced until the glass is cold when it can be safely taken out. With heavy pieces this cooling process can take two or three days according to the size of the piece. I usually work on fine wine glasses and goblets and the tempering takes much less time. Usually we close the *tempera* at about 2 or 2.30 in the afternoon and it is opened at about 3 in the morning when all the pieces are taken out.

A goblet like this one which must be fifteen inches tall would take me about half an hour to make. *Momento, momento!* I mean it would take half an hour to form the glass. But I did not make it alone. As I was saying a *maestro* always needs help. First I made the bowl, then the stem and then the foot and then one uses heat to fuse the three together. Then, after it had been tempered, the glass was engraved by other hands. Not by me. I am not an engraver. I do not know that craft. It is a beautiful piece. It turned out well.

Now this flask made in the traditional red of Venetian glass with traditional ornamentation in gold, I made just before the summer holidays. I only made three. One is on show at the factory, one the director of our works took home with him and the third one he gave to me. I think that was a very nice gesture, don't you?

The number of helpers a *maestro* needs depends entirely on what he is working and they are not always the same helpers. For instance, today I needed twelve assistants to make a single glass. When we are glass-blowing everything is quiet, everyone concentrated, there is no idle chat to distract from the alertness required from everyone. Everybody knows his job. I never have to say, "Do this. Fetch that." They are all good, capable boys. They know the job and are just as interested as I am in turning out something well-made and beautiful. These assistants, by watching and doing, learn. There is now a school which gives a preliminary training but it is really experience which counts. There were no schools for glass-blowers in my time. I learnt all I know from the *maestri* I worked with — and by experience. Experience is the essential thing.

When you buy glass in Venice you have to be very careful because a lot of it is not Murano glass at all. Some of it is very good, good crystal and good workmanship, but it comes from Tuscany or some other place. It is not Murano glass and if you want this, and want to be sure you are getting it, you must go to a glass factory in Murano and buy it direct.

I went to school here in Burano. Of course that was the time of fascism. That was the ruination of Italy and the war was on as well. When I was ten I was brought face to face with fascist behaviour. There was a group of fascists sent here to Burano to make a round up of suspects. My friend and I were in our boat when suddenly two young men who were trying to escape from the fascists seized our boat, threw us out into the water and rowed off as fast as they could. My friend and I, very frightened, were just scrambling on shore when the fascists arrived on the quay. When they saw that the young men were likely to slip through their fingers they started firing on them and killed them both. I can still see it. It was a terrible thing. That was in 1943 and I was just ten. Those fascists were not Buranelli. They always sent in people from outside to do this kind of thing. I was ten. It was a frightful thing for a little boy to see.

In those days there was no junior secondary school here and pupils had to travel every day to Venice. I had really set my heart on going on with my schooling but it couldn't be done. The war was still on and it was not possible to send a child of ten off alone to Venice all day by *vaporetto*. And, anyway, there were difficulties at home. We were seven brothers and very often there was practically nothing to eat at home. That is another consequence of fascism. Fascism leads to nothing but hunger and misery. So I did not go to school and became a fisherman instead. I did not like it and I went on dreaming about going back to school. But I went on being a fisherman until the end of the war and then I helped my father who was a *bagnino* (attendant in charge of bathing at a beach) and at the end of 1945 I got a job in a glassworks and I have been there ever since and now you know about the whole of my life!

When I became a glass-worker I started to earn, not very much, but I had a little money left over from what I gave to my mother and then I went back to school — only in the evening — and this time to do music. At that time I was earning about two thousand lire a week and out of this I managed to keep three hundred litre which was just enough to pay for one private lesson a week. Three of us joined together for these lessons, my brother who played the clarinet, my friend who played the trumpet and I who then played the clarinet and the saxophone. So I had at last got my way, and was studying again. I have always loved music. I think one either has a feeling for it or not. It is all or nothing. As soon as we could we formed ourselves into a little group and on Saturday and Sunday we used to play at dances, and weddings and reunions, at anything we could get so that we could pay for more lessons and better instruments. At about this time I started playing the piano. So that was how we solved our financial problems. Of course we could never go to a music college because we were at our jobs all day and so we could not take any diplomas but that did not matter. We didn't want pieces of paper, we wanted music. I remember I used to eat my supper sitting at table on the piano-stool so as not to waste any time getting to the piano. I just twiddled round and started right off.

One of my friends who used to teach the clarinet and I later founded our little orchestra here. We started it about twelve years ago, perhaps fifteen, and I have always been the *maestro* (conductor). We called the orchestra after one of our Burano citizens who is very well known: the musician Baldassarre Galuppi, who was nicknamed Il Buranello. We give little concerts and we accompany little choirs here and in Venice. Yesterday we were in Cavallino playing for an Old Comrades' Association. We play a lot at this sort of ex-servicemen's and military ceremony which chiefly means the national anthem, the Last Post, all that sort of stuff. Then, of course, we also play more light-hearted pieces, little marches and other suitable things when people are enjoying themselves in large groups. Mostly we play the work of well-known musicians but there is always some friend in the orchestra who has written a little piece and we usually find an opportunity of playing it. The driver of the *mototopo* who used to come by your house in Torcello every morning playing the trombone is one of the best players in the orchestra and he has also composed several good pieces. Apart from our concerts there is no music here in Burano. There are very occasionally concerts in Torcello. We recently went to one, a marvellous occasion. Just think, Bach and Galuppi in the setting of the Basilica of Torcello!

One of the important things the orchestra does is to encourage young people here to take an interest in music and give them a chance to develop it. Of course it also helps us if we can find young people who will really work at an instrument and then join us. So a number of us teach in our spare time. Of course we do not charge anything. We do it for the children and for the orchestra. Now we have one little girl aged nine. She is the only girl who has ever wanted to join the orchestra and we hope that she will bring us others. I am teaching her the rudiments at present and the beginnings of the flute. Another way we encourage the children is to provide instruments. I don't mean we lend them an instrument. We buy them one if they seem to have a gift and be serious about learning and then it is their own. We are of course paid, not much but a little always, for the concerts we give but none of it goes into the pockets of the players. We all play for love of it, and the money goes towards our expenses and buying instruments for the young ones. The results of all this has been that the orchestra has got some really good young players and we have the satisfaction of having helped them. We have one boy who is in his fourth year at the Music College in Venice studying the trombone, another in his third year whose instrument is the clarinet, and a younger boy in his second year, again the trombone. We are very happy with the results and I think they are too. They are all local boys and just appeared one day, like this little girl, and asked if they could learn music and whatever instrument they have taken a liking to. We do not get any help from anyone. The Venice municipality would like to help us but it seems it can't or, at least, that is what it says.

Life, material life, is very much better in Burano than it used to be when I was a boy. Before the war the people were very poor and unhealthy. Tuberculosis in particular was very widespread, probably because of housing conditions. If you have ten people sleeping in the same room naturally infectious diseases spread. It is quite wrong to think that fishermen and people who work out of doors all day do not get these illnesses. Glass-workers too used to be frequently ill, pneumonia mostly, but that was because of the heat of the furnaces and the contrast with the outside temperature in winter. But now we have good, properly heated *motonave* (motorships) which are big enough to take us all from Murano to Burano without too much overcrowding. And of course with better wages and more employment the people are better fed and, if they do fall ill, there is better medical attention.

We have had piped water for about ten years now. Before that we had to depend on wells. They were mostly in the *campielli* (courtyards) and you had to go out and fetch it. The water was not bad but not as good as we get now. The water in Mazzorbo was really brackish and unpleasant and the people over there were very glad when they got good water. Now we have good sanitation too. You have to pay for it yourself but nearly everybody has installed it. The houses are small and built before the days of bathrooms but you can always find a corner in even the smallest house. It is really a question of whether you want to spend the money.

Life is certainly better. There is more work. Even in this difficult time there is not too much unemployment. So far at least, nobody in the Murano glassworks has been laid off for more than about three weeks in the year and that is not death.'

*

The second glass-worker was a much older man who grew up in great adversity but managed to complete his primary school leaving certificate by attending night school. This is what he had to say:

'My real troubles began when I went to work, because I hadn't got an employment card. I wasn't old enough. At that time you could get a card at twelve and when I started I wasn't yet twelve. When I started work I must have been about ten. My first job was in a glass factory in Murano, one of the big ones which produced all sorts of articles and had a huge capital behind it. When the commissioners of the labour office came round to see that all the regulations were being observed, the director used to send word down to the foreman to hide us boys so that the commissioners did not see us. They hid us, just imagine that!

We used to go to work in boats, rowing boats, mind you, there were no *vaporetti* then. We had to row all the way from Burano to Murano. How long did it take? Well, that depended on the weather and the wind and tide. Some days it could take up to two or three hours. And then after a day's work in the heat of the furnaces we had to pick up our oars again and row all the way home. Some firms used to make arrangements with the owners of *sandali* and all the workers

89

who used them contributed to what it cost the firm to hire them. And so quite a lot of us used to go to work that way. But the trouble was that you got so cold in the winter, just sitting in the boat doing nothing after a day by the furnaces. You had to be very careful to wrap up if you didn't want to catch pneumonia.

We did not earn much at that time. Later when I was older I used to get five lire a day and that was not enough to live on. When I had finished my military service (I am of the 1906 class so I did my service in 1926 and finished in 1927), I was getting a hundred lire a week. That must have been in 1928 or 1929. You had to pinch to live on that. It was a grim time, really grim. You had to choose between eating at mid-day and eating at night. We did not starve but there was only money for one meal a day. Mostly we ate *polenta* (a stiff kind of porridge made with maize) and fish or *pasta* with beans. Nothing else. Meat? Eh! We very rarely saw meat! Meat was something for the grand people. Meat, chicken and all that was for them. But we had wine, enough wine. There was no shortage of wine. But as for a bit of luxury, as for eating like the well-off people, nothing doing.

So my life went on like this till, with the passage of time, and by doing my best to learn more, I became a skilled worker. I became a temperer in the glass factory. It was my job to regulate the temperature of the cooling oven where the newly-blown glass articles were put. You see, if you put the hot glass into the air it shatters. You have to temper it just as you temper steel, and you do it by putting the articles into ovens regulated to whatever heat is required for however long is required by the particular type of article you are tempering and then reducing the heat very gradually. And after a time, it may be a few hours or a day or two, depending on the article, you can safely take them out into the air. Of course all this work of maintaining and controlling the heat is done mechanically nowadays. In my time everything was done by hand. One used coke. You know that lightweight coal, Cardiff coke they called it because it came from Cardiff. You had constantly to watch the temperature and shovel on coke. The oven is a kind of tunnel ten or fifteen metres long and first you have to put the trolleys which hold the glass articles into the oven to get hot because of course you cannot temper articles properly if you stand them on a cold surface. It was my responsibility to judge the various degrees of heat required for the different objects and the length of time needed, and we learnt to do it by experience, by long experience. I got my experience as an apprentice. My first job was to haul the trolleys in and out of the oven with a winding handle and a chain. When the trolleys were ready the temperer rang a bell, an old-fashioned bell with a clapper, you know? Then the finisher came along and with a special sort of fork he picked up each article and placed them on the trolley, all standing upright. I did all the jobs round the furnace and bit by bit I learnt all the trade of a temperer. Later they installed oil-fired furnaces and now they are mostly heated by electricity and the various degrees of heat are controlled by thermostats. You wait till it shows the heat you want and *boop*! There you are! It is easier, certainly, and the work is less hard. Beautiful these new things are but we worked always by experience.

Mostly the glass was blown but the factory also made moulded glass, machine-made, in fact. You can always tell moulded glass by running your finger along it and you will feel a little ridge where the mould joins. Blown glass never has this little ridge. There are now many techniques of making glass. In Murano they now make a lot of machine-made glass, bottles, glasses of all kinds and those big demijohns for wine, and in many different colours and also in that pretty smoky tint. Besides this there is the artistic side of the works. There, of course, it is mostly blown glass. They make fine, light, wonderful things as well as solid, heavy things in splendid colours, like those ash-trays.

When I was a fully qualified temperer I got 120 lire a week. It was possible to live, just possible with care. It was a bit tight but the cost of living, relative to our earnings, was lower than today. Nowadays they pay well. If you have the will to work you can live well. You can see that from the houses here in Burano. Look at any house. It is comfortable, well-appointed, nicely furnished. *Bella, in somma!* And it is all due to the increase in wages and jobs after the war. Of course there were crises, but on the whole things have got much better since the war. Now we are in a critical period, but it isn't only national, it's everywhere, look at England, look at the United States. So far we haven't had much unemployment in Burano.

The population has recently gone down a bit. We are about 6,000 now. Some people have moved out to better housing. Until a little while ago we didn't even have proper sanitation. Now the sewage is properly dealt with. It doesn't go into the lagoon — at least not till it is purified. There aren't any more *pozzi morti* but proper sanitary arrangements. Of course people paid for these improvements themselves. When they began to be properly paid after the war and when they had bought their houses they wanted better conditions. Naturally there are still a few families who won't spend the money. They still stick to the old ways — old oilcans mostly — and they sneak out very early when nobody is around and tip it into the canal. The stink, my goodness! Particularly at low tide. Of course if they get caught they are heavily fined and you can imagine how the neighbours complain and the sanitary inspectors are after them all the time. But luckily there are very few of them and getting fewer every day. Everybody dislikes them for their filthy ways. We are clean people here and we take great pride in our pretty houses.

We have had electricity for a long time now but lighting was a problem when I was a boy. I loved reading and I used to read by the light of a paraffin lamp or a candle. I remember when I was about twelve reading *The Count of Monte Cristo*. Yes, I was about twelve when I read that, and *Les Misérables* and *The Three Musketeers* by Dumas, Alexander Dumas that is, and several other of his stories and also others by Hugo. I did enjoy reading. I always have. You know, my schooling only took me up to the fifth class [the first five years of the primary level]. Now, just you listen to this. I left school at the end of the third year because I had to start earning. I was recalled in 1939 into the Alpine Regiment — at the time that Albania was occupied and they made Victor-Emmanuel, that clown, an emperor, just imagine! And then you know how he abandoned Italy and took himself off. But all that has become history. As I was saying, I was recalled then but only served for six months and then came home. Now, in 1939 I got married, no, no, that is wrong. In 1939 I got engaged and in 1940 I got married. Now I've got it right. We had to think ahead, to think seriously about the future, and my wife (but she was my fiancée then) agreed not to get married until I had a job under some government department so as to be sure of having at least a good plate of soup every day. A friend finally got me a steady job and there I stayed for years and worked myself up to a modest situation. I really did want to get on. I have always wanted to get on. Who was it who said "he who desires greatly, desires victoriously"? Alfieri, wasn't it? Vittorio Alfieri, a great poet. And then there is that other phrase: "Three times in the dust, three times to the heights." Now, the fellow who said that was Napoleon, wasn't it? I think it was. From that time, from the time I got that job my life changed. See how things change. From times of vicissitudes and difficulties, bit by bit, thanks to modern advances and fighting for our rights and the growth of the trade unions and by strike action (mind you, I only joined in economic strikes. I don't hold with strikes of a political character. Economic strikes are essential sometimes if one is not going to allow oneself to be treated as a worm) things have altered for the better. Now I am a pensioner. I have two pensions and as there is only my wife and myself we manage. Unfortunately I have to pay rent but it is not too much because it is a controlled rent. I pay 16,000 lire a month.

Now, to go back to that bit about desiring something greatly. I began my job under this government department as a labourer but I said to myself, why should I always give way to others, I want to get on. So gradually I climbed up and one day I had an opportunity to become a security guard. Security guards have to carry arms and to take an oath, and the regulations lay down that you cannot do this unless you have passed the fifth class. And I had only got as far as the third. So I went back to school, to night school, although I was getting on by then, and made up those two years and was able to take the oath and bear arms and became a security guard. So you see if you want enough to get ahead you do succeed. Alfieri was right.'

93

Burano lace, so delicate, so light that it is called *punto in aria* (a stitch in the air), dates back to the Buranello sailor who, sailing along between the island of Capri and the mainland where the Sirens sang, refused to stop his ears or be tied to the mast like Ulysses because he loved his girl so much that no enchantment could in the least affect him. The Queen of the Sirens heard of this and sent her singers with the most alluring voices to swim singing round his ship. He smiled at them and sailed on. She then went to sing to him herself, singing her most beguiling songs in her most melodious voice. He was greatly moved and bowed and smiled and . . . sailed on. Half in irritation and half in admiration for his great love and constancy she sent a wave splashing over him as he stood in the prow of his ship. The spray solidified as it fell round his feet and when he took it in his hands he found it retained a gossamer-cohesion. Such fine work, such lightness, such intricacy had never been seen before and he gave it to his bride to use as a wedding veil. The other marriageable girls of Burano became so envious that they determined to copy the miraculous work of the veil the sailor had given his bride. They succeeded so well that the *punto buranese*, the *punto in aria*, was created.

Some more solemn historians claim that lace-making originated in Byzantine times on the not too impressive evidence that the *punto in aria* uses many of the same decorative themes found in early mosaics or stone carvings. But these still exist in Torcello and, earlier, existed in many conventual churches which have long since disappeared into the lagoon, and which could have inspired the designs of the lace-makers at any point in time.

The first trustworthy references to lace-making date from the fifteenth century. Venice, and more particularly Burano, became the centre of this new craft. Tradition has it that the manufacture of lace was given great impetus by Giovanna Malipiero who was dogess in 1457 and certainly by another dogess, Morosina Morosini Grimani, the wife of Marino Grimani (doge in 1595), who at her own expense set up a lace-making centre and provided all the materials and instruments required by the 130 women who worked under the direction of Mistress Cattina Gardin. This centre was closed down on the death of Morosina Morosini Grimani but the industry continued to flourish. *Punto in aria, punto buranese,* Venetian point, the lace made here, by whatever name it was known, became greatly sought after all over Europe as

personal adornment, as well as for altar cloths and ecclesiastical robes. It was also copied. Colbert, Louis XIV's great minister of finance, encouraged the craft in France and lured away women from Burano to teach French women how to make what became known chiefly as *point d'Alençon*. The Buranelli were ordered home by a jealous Venetian government, ever ready to protect its commercial secrets, but lace-making was launched in Europe and made its triumphant way in many countries.

Two techniques of lace-making originated in the lagoon. The lace made in Burano was first known as *punto tagliato* which seems to indicate that lace began as embroidery carried one step further. The design to be followed by the lace-maker was (and, indeed, still is) stitched on to a stout piece of cloth which in turn was fixed for convenience of working on to a little pillow which was held in the lace-maker's lap. When the design had been completely stitched it was cut off from the supporting cloth from behind so that the whole was held together only by its own stitches. This light, delicate, unsupported network became known as *punto in aria*. There are six stitches used in *punto in aria*. They are the *ghipuer*, the *sbarri* and the *rete* which form the skeleton of the lace and are done in the order given over the whole piece. Then come the *rilievo* or raised stitches which are the *smerli*, *picco* and *grossi*, also done in this order.

The other technique of lace-making developed in the lagoon was to use not the needle but bobbins. A skilled worker flicks these to and fro and knots them into intricate patterns with breath-taking speed and skill. This technique was also developed very early and was introduced into Germany and the Low Countries by Venetian merchants as early as 1536. It still flourishes in Bruges. In the lagoon its home is Pellestrina. This little fishing port on the lagoon side of the narrow Murazzi has not the reputation among tourists which Burano probably acquired quite fortuitously because it is the neighbour of Torcello and its magnificent monuments. The stall-holders and shops of Burano still commission work from the lace-makers to supply the tourist trade. Pellestrina has no tourist trade and is mostly interesting as giving a glimpse of what Burano itself must have looked like before reasonable wages and relative security brought it a measure of prosperity. So the two or three old women of Pellestrina who still make lace with their pillows and bobbins try, rather desperately, to sell their work direct, and for derisory prices, to the very few visitors whose curiosity takes them to this shabby, unkempt little fishing port.

Apparently lace-making, whether in Burano or Pellestrina, was never organised or given statutes, which seems odd for so valuable an industry in a city as pertinaciously and minutely administered as Venice. Perhaps this was because it must always have been a cottage industry depending on the work of women in their homes. This too may have been one of the reasons for its decline in the nineteenth century.

It was a very difficult century for Venice. The slow collapse of the Serene Republic, so long lethargic in commerce and spendthrift of its accumulated wealth of centuries, ended with its humiliating destruction by Napoleon, and the years of Austrian occupation and of struggle to join the new Italy of the Risorgimento did nothing to help its economic recovery. The difficulties for the poor areas — and Burano was one of the poorest — were increased with the invention of mechanical means of making lace. By the end of the century there was not only no lace being made, the knowledge of the craft of lace-making had practically disappeared. That it did not was due to the efforts of two philanthropic Venetians, Paulo Fambri and the Contessa Adriana Marcello who in an attempt to alleviate the penury into which Burano had fallen sought out the only old woman, the seventy year old Cencia Scarpariola, who still remembered the secrets of making *punto in aria*, and set up a lace-school to teach the craft to women and girls. The school and the little museum attached to it kept the craft alive and provided work and a livelihood for several generations of Burano women.

By the 1960s the economic situation in Burano had changed radically for the better. There was now a range of jobs for women offering better and more regular money than they could obtain by making lace. Consequently attendance at the lace-school declined and early in the 1970s the school closed for lack of pupils.

Now an attempt is being made to re-open it. It was a miracle that life could be infused into the school in the last years of the nineteenth century. One must wonder whether it is wise in the last quarter of the twentieth century to seek a repetition of the miracle. Nobody of any sensibility would wish to see a craft die. But does it help crafts to keep them alive for purely antiquarian motives, as curiosities, as *roba di touristi* (tourist gimmicks) without any real economic vitality? Should one regret the passing of chain-mail armour or the velocipede? Can lace have any more relevance to our lives?

The first of the lace-makers to talk about her work was an old woman of indestructible gaiety and industry. Almost every conversational turn was illustrated by a snatch of song. She began with a song:

> 'Eh, chi non lavora
> Non fa l'amore
> Questo mi ha detto
> Ieri mia mamma.'*

Mia mamma, mia mamma, it was many years ago that my mother told me that. I am seventy-seven, seven, seven, and all my life I have made lace. They say that life is a waltz. It is not true! (Sings) *La vita non è che un valse†*; how does it go, how does it go? I forget. Yes, I am a Buranella, born here, married here to a Buranello, and making lace all the time. This is the lace-pillow I always use. You see how I work? I attach the piece I am working on to it and inside, in this little drawer, I keep all the things I need, skeins of thread, scissors, needles and powder for my hands, They need to be clean and dry. It would never do to get the needle all sweaty and the lace dirty. Look, I've just been paid 700 lire. One and a half days that piece took me. Five hundred lire a day is what I reckon to make. This bit on my cushion now. My part of it will take me four days. I do not make the whole of it. I only do these bars across here and round here. Four days' work at 500 lire a day. I work from seven in the morning till seven at night. Some cannot do it, their eyes won't stand it. I wear glasses, I have done for years now and I can work long hours with glasses. Anyway I have got to. I am all alone now. I've no father, no mother, no husband. Yes, I have a room in my son's house and I earn what I need by making lace. I get enough for a bit of bread and soup and a bit of butter and

*Oh, those who do not work do not make love. So my mother told me yesterday.
†Life is not only a waltz.

sometimes cheese — and fish, of course.

It was my mother who taught me how to make lace. Usually it was the mothers who taught their girls and then they went ahead and found work for themselves. I taught my daughter all I knew and so it goes on from generation to generation. Now, I am not sure if it will go on. This girl here, she is still at school doing her junior secondary and, as you can see, she is already quite good, but when she gets through school (she is not old enough to leave yet) but as soon as she is old enough she will leave and go into a glassworks, packing glass probably, they usually use girls for packing the glass, and she will get a good day's pay for her work. I don't think the girls now would want just to make lace even if they could earn a living at it. They make lace for themselves, for their bottom drawers, for when they get married:

> Come un sogno d'or
> Palpita nel mio cuor
> Hi ricordo ancor
> Di quel amor che non esiste piu.*

All the girls nowadays go into the glass factories because they are paid a decent day's wage. I get 500 lire a day. It is not worth the effort. (Sings) *Guarda Maria com'è bella†* oh dear, I have lost my memory. I cannot remember a thing. I have always loved singing . . . (A neighbour breaking into the conversation: "When her brother died, she did not even know when they took him away. And she started to sing . . ."). Eh, well, you know, there are characters like that. It didn't mean I didn't love my brother. I don't know when I am singing and when I am not . . . But this girl, she makes a bit of lace now, she earns enough to dress herself. She'll make lace until she is old enough to work in a factory. Then she will be paid properly for a day's work. No 500 lire a day for her! Anyway the lace school is closed now. It has been closed for three years. None of the girls want to go there. But in the glass-works they get paid for a day's work.

When we old women are gone the art of lace-making will die. It is disappearing already as you can see. Nearly all of us

*My heart trembles like a golden dream. I still remember that love which no more exists.
†See now beautiful Maria is.

lace-makers are old. Look at me, seventy-seven and 500 lire a day!

Una volta c'era l'abbondanza
Che ci faceva un po' di vita bella*'

*

The second lace-maker was also an old woman. She was a little dour, somewhat burdened with recollections of past hardships but her talk was now and again lit by flashes of an earthy humour. This is what she said:

'We did not have any electric light when I was young. We used to take a glass or a cup or something and pour a little oil in it and dip the wick in and with this little light we went about the house and lived after dark. The little oil lamp gave out about as much light as a candle. And to keep ourselves warm in winter we had *scaldini*. They were little bronze pots and you lit a bit of charcoal in them to heat them up. The old women used to put them under their skirts — you know their skirts used to come down to the ground — well, they put their skirts over them to keep their feet warm. And that was our only heating: some people did use wood, but that was mostly for cooking. It cost too much to use for heating. But before we had bottled gas we used to cook with wood. It used to be delivered in big boats, *piatte* we called them. We all had to buy wood. We were not like the people on the *terraferma* who always had enough wood growing on their land. There is no wood growing here in Burano. And before we had water from the aquaduct we depended on wells for all our water. Now we have enough water and we have proper lavatories, water closets like everybody else. Before then, what did we have? Buckets! Like old Noah in his ark. He had a bucket. And some of us had *bidoni* (oil cans), *bidoni* (cackling), *bidoni* and some still do!

I remember one very, very cold winter the Franciscan fathers came over from the Desert walking on the ice all the way. *Si, Si,* they walked on the ice all the way from San

*Once upon a time there was plenty which made our lives pleasant.

100

Francesco del Deserto to here in Burano. It was a dreadfully cold winter that. What a thing! I must have been seven or eight years old at the time. I have heard that the lagoon was frozen all the way between here and Venice. But I don't know about that. What I do remember is that the fathers walked over from the Desert. I remember because I was in bed with influenza and my *mamma* came in and said: "Look at that priest, walking on the ice!" It must have been 1929 when I saw about twenty of the fathers walking across on the ice.

Then about ten years ago we had that great flood, the *acqua alta* here in Burano. The water was so high that we went up and down the *calli* in boats and even across the *piazza*, everywhere.

My grandfather was a *guardian di valli* (in charge of an enclosure for rearing fish). My father was a carpenter and my mother was a teacher of lace-making. She began to teach me when I was about eight years old. I worked like this, making lace with a needle (we do not use bobbins here: they say they use bobbins in Pellestrina, but I have never been there) and using a lace pillow, just as I do now. I have always made lace, never embroidery or anything else, always *punto di Burano* lace. There were twelve of us at home, half girls and half boys. My *papa* and *mamma*, my aunt, grandfather and grandmother, and we all lived in the house where Romano's restaurant is now. My mother ran the lace school downstairs. She had three hundred women working for her. Of course she did not own the school, she just ran it. The nuns owned the school and they lived upstairs. I was taught to do all the stitches, *tutti, tutti, tutti*. Many lace-makers specialise in one or other of the stitches but I like to do the whole of a piece of work myself. I like to begin and end a piece. I get more satisfaction doing a whole piece all alone. I have always worked even after I married. When I got married I said I wanted ten children, and I really did. And what happened? I only got two and I wanted ten. But destiny decided on two. But these two are good, very good. Both married.

Before the war there was such poverty here. Mostly the men were fishermen. They earned little, so little. Now the men mostly work in the glass factories in Murano or as *bagnini* (beach attendants). With these big hotels and caravan sites all along the coast towards Jesolo they need many *bagnini*. The jobs continue all the year round because there are always things to do: cabins to be repaired and painted and got ready for the summer season.'

*

The third lace-maker was much younger. She was married to an unskilled labourer and the little she earned was valuable in the house. She said:

'This work has taken me a week and I get 2,000 lire for it. I started it last Saturday and I shall finish it today, Saturday. I do not work all day, of course. I have my house to see to and my family to look after and meals to get but in the afternoons I usually come out here for a few hours with my friends and we make lace and chat together. Even if I had time I could not work many more hours because lace-making is hard on the eyes. No, I don't wear glasses to work — not yet. But then I am much younger than most lace-workers.

It is not possible to make a living out of lace-making but, given my circumstances, we do not have much money coming in, I can buy a few things we need — a pair of clogs, for instance (we need clogs with all this water about). It is just a little supplement to my husband's wages. So now you see why the girls do not want to learn to make lace.

We are each given work mostly by the people who sell the lace, sometimes by ladies who want lace for themselves. They give us the pattern all stitched out on a piece of coarse backing cloth and also the thread and we do whatever stitches we are best at. They offer so much for the work, we discuss it and come to an agreement on the price.

We were six children at home. Families are smaller now. I only have four. But even with a smaller family it is difficult, particularly just now. My daughter who is eighteen has been unemployed for five months. The glassworks are closing or going on short time. They try not to dismiss men with families so it becomes even more difficult for the young ones who are just beginning. It is not so much that the price of

102

glass objects has gone up. It is the export trade that has dropped.

I never went to school if I could help it. The schoolmistress was always coming round to complain to my mother. I used to like skipping. I used to spend my life skipping. My children though have always liked school. The eldest went up to the third year of junior secondary, the second up to the first year and the next is in her second year now and will do her third year next year. And one is still in primary school. All went very willingly to school not like their *mamma*, but you know I don't miss it much, being educated I mean.

We go shopping two or three times a day. Well, people like to eat so we go out and buy it. It depends too on how much money you have got in your pocket. It is no good going shopping without any money. Then I have always forgotten something, the parsley or the carrots, and I have to go out again. Then it is nice to take a little walk, to get out of the house and see your friends.'

The Padrone of Romano's

Romano's restaurant, whose proper name is *Le Tre Stelle*, stands half-way along the via Baldassare Galuppi between the wooden bridge and the Fondamenta dei Assassini at one end and the Piazza at the other. In summer an awning protects its green-painted front and tables are set out in its shade. Inside is a large room divided down the middle by two rows of columns supporting red and green beams decorated with copper fish and other sea creatures. On one side of the passage so created and fenced off by green wooden plant stands, usually bereft of plants, is the restaurant side of the room with comfortably large tables laid with neat white cloths. Except when there is a great press of business or a wedding luncheon the tables on the other side are left bare and the place is used as a meeting place, a sort of exchange for chat by fishermen and other Buranelli. Towards the back, on this side, is a long bar and, usually, at the end of this, convenient to the telephone and the cash-desk and with the arch leading to the kitchen immediately at his left hand, stands *il padrone* (the owner, the master, mine host, as you prefer). This little space is indeed his quarter-deck from which he can command every activity and every part of the restaurant, except the long interior room which runs back to the courtyard where, more often than not, you will find that a painter has set up his easel. The walls of both these rooms are crowded with paintings, drawings, photographs and press cuttings. Most of the paintings are by members of what has become known as the Buranello school and have been presented by the painters to the *padrone* or to his father who was the Romano by whose name the place is

known. In the centre of one wall there is a case with a decorated pediment and the words 'La Baracola' picked out in gold. La Baracola is much more than a rowing club devoted to encourage a sport. It is more a fraternal association which helps its members in many ways, particularly in time of trouble. This case contains the pennants, the battle honours won over the years by members of La Baracola at the annual Venice regatta. The two most famous oarsmen are Albino dei Rossi, known as Strighetta (Little Witch) and Marcello Bon, known as Giapate (the Grabber). Beside the case of pennants hang two illuminated certificates presented by the Venetian municipality to each of these stalwarts on their winning their fifth championship. Photographs of the famous sitting happily at tables loaded with fish and wine include one of Prince Philip, as he was then, and one of Charlie Chaplin. The press cuttings extol the paintings, the cooking, the rowing and the *ambiance.*

Romano's is seen at its best on a winter's day. From the open kitchen there comes a gentle sizzle of frying and low voices as *la mamma* ordains, organises and produces each customer's requirements. The waiters, old hands every one, are not too busy to exchange a word with regular diners on their respective healths and families or to whisper a recommendation — the sole, today, some *gentili* have come in. The fish on its oval dish is never too much or too little. How does *la mamma* know just how hungry one is, just how much fish *risotto* one can eat? And then comes the *fritto misto*, a little sole, a small piece of eel (a soupçon too much would ruin the dish), a few *scampi*, a few squidlets delicately browned and the whole accompanied by a great jug of white wine.

In winter there is a scattering of guests. There are a few foreigners. Some French out-of-season lovers, so nice, so cosy, so egotistical and so happy, at least for the moment. A group of American students with a guidebook on Italy on five dollars a day (they must have left home a long time ago and their clothes rather underscore the fact) deposit their rucksacks and anxiously consult the menu and the waiter and sorrowfully load up again and disappear unobtrusively while he tidies the table once more. Neatly, courteously done and honour saved on both sides. But how sad that they should have to munch a bun on the quay when they had had high hopes of Romano's cooking. Over there sits a Venetian, a character out of a Longhi painting with a rather heavy face supported by five chins and a red jersey. Here two Venetian ladies, the older, with a complicated 1890s hairdo, expertly wrings the neck of a roll and offers a mutilated half to the younger, groomed as only an Italian hairdresser knows how. There is an air of conspiracy at every table. If one were near enough one would know that they were discussing installing a new bathroom or the imminent arrival of somebody's baby but, inevitably, being Venetian, they give the impression that they are plotting to reverse the government, explode a bomb or, being so remote from the modern world, taking steps to oust the Austrian occupiers — it is so in Florian's and Harry's Bar and Montin's and any café round any corner and it is so at Romano's also. This is best seen as a winter phenomenon. It is masked but by no means eradicated by the presence of a myriad summer visitors.

In the meantime on the other side of the columns the volume of talk has been rising as the men (this is exclusively a man's world) wander in. The drinking is done standing at the bar and seldom goes beyond a glass of wine. Your Buranello is frugal as well as poor. Sometimes one of them will order a number of drinks and will personally plunk them down firmly in front of the friends he is treating. At other tables sit men reading newspapers or filling up their football pools with much licking of pencils. There is a good cross-section of Burano in here, the tidy and the unkempt, the aged and the young, the bandy (who suddenly become statuesque rowing a boat) and the straight. There are overcoats and anoraks, overalls, jerseys and fur hats with earflaps. There is a little pushing and horseplay, all very amiable and certainly nothing to attract a reproving glance from the quarter-deck. They are all at home here however unkempt, undisciplined, respectable, ugly, admirable, proud, reserved, independent, and a few are a little bit nasty perhaps. If you live a difficult life maybe you have to become a little bit nasty to stay alive. This seems to be reflected in their behaviour to one man. He is a well-known local. He spends his life in and out of gaol, but not because he has committed any great crimes. He is a stupid little man with a bad temper which gets him into trouble. He comes in boldly enough but is totally ignored and has to sit at a table by himself. He speaks to one of the foreigners sitting on the edge of the restaurant side and is sent a drink. He tries for another and is refused and sees the waiter's eye is on him. For the men on his side of the room he simply does not exist. There is not a glance, not a flicker of interest when he comes in or when he goes out. His offence cannot be that he has been in gaol, Burano is too broad-minded a place for that. But he has clearly committed some crime which the community is not prepared to overlook and it has rubbed him out.

This is Romano's in the winter. In the summer you will rub shoulders with Venice and with the world, with film-stars and hippies, with the overdressed and the practically bare, with the learned, the pretentious, the intelligent, the dim and those who simply love the place.

This is what the *padrone* said:

'My family first got a trading licence eighty or ninety years ago but the business as it now is was worked up by my father who took over about sixty years ago. The business has always been in the family but at first we ran it partly as an *osteria* (inn) where we let rooms as well as providing meals. We also sold dye for fishing nets, equipment for sportsmen, that is to say, for shooting and fishing. It was a mixed family trading business, you understand. Then gradually we specialised as a restaurant.

The Romano of the restaurant's name was my father, though everybody still knows us by that name. Our family name is Barbaro. I am not called Romano. I am called Orazio — Orazio Barbaro — and my grandfather who started the family business was called Angelo. But the restaurant really started to expand under my father which is why it became known as Romano's. It is actually called the Three Stars, not that anybody ever calls it that.

It must have been in the 1920s that painters started coming to us such as Mario Vellani Marchi who became a friend of my father's and gave him a painting. That was the beginning of this collection of paintings which hang in the restaurant. They have been given to my father and now they are mine. The first of them, as I said, was Mario Vellani Marchi who broke his thigh two years ago and has not been able to come out to us since then. This is very sad for me because he is like a father to me. It was he and his friends who created the atmosphere of this place. He and the others made a sort of clubhouse of the restaurant. Gradually others like Silvio Consadori, Luigi Brambati, Gino Rossi, Savino Labo, Pio Semeghini, and others whom you can often see working in the garden over there. Apart from all the pictures down here we have another eighty or ninety upstairs where we live.

107

They are in the living rooms and the bedrooms and on all the walls everywhere. The place is full of them, you see. Then we became quite well known and newspaper articles were written about us and this drew famous people to the restaurant. The Duke of Edinburgh came here as a young man. That must have been in 1951, I suppose. He was still Prince Philip in those days. There is his photograph with my wife. Luigi Einaudi, the President of Italy, came at about the same time. Many theatre and film people, such as Charlie Chaplin, and literary people like Hemingway and Sinclair Lewis. Earlier on we had many military people here during the Fascist period and during the war when the Germans garrisoned the forts out here in the lagoon. Then the partisans came over from the *terraferma* and occupied the forts when the Germans had left in a hurry and still later there were American soldiers. We have had General MacArthur here. And naturally we still get famous people of today.

I have always worked here, always. First I helped my father and for the last eleven years, since he died in fact, I have run it myself. The kitchen is in the charge of *la mamma*, that is to say my wife, but everybody calls her *la mamma*. Then I have two daughters. The older one is already working with us in the kitchen. She is nearly nineteen. The younger one is still studying, mostly book-keeping and accounting. The older one did not want to go on with school and preferred to work with us here at home. She is a great help and is becoming pretty good at cooking certain things. Her fish *risotto* is really good and that is a very important speciality of ours, as you know. She is really interested and it seems to be working out well. Our staff is not very large here and we do not have to go looking round the streets to get them. One of our waiters has been with us for twenty-eight years, another twenty-four and another eighteen. We are a family. There is no question of master *(padrone)* and man here. We are all equal, all one family. They are far too faithful ever to abandon Romano's. We all live together and when we go away one or other of them keeps an eye on things.

I have always liked working here in Burano. I have always had a passion for this place and the lagoon. It is a marvellous place for painting. I love Burano, it is my life. I got this love by inheritance, you understand! When I return from a trip and see my crooked *campanile* I know I am all right. I begin to breathe again. I am home. I love this island of ours. We are like that, we Buranelli, we like to stay here in our island.

Some people had to leave the island, but very regretfully, because they had to find somewhere to live. There is no possibility of increasing housing here. There is no room to expand. So they had to go, some to Treporti, the nearest available place to Burano, over in the Cavalino peninsula, and a few to Venice or to Mestre. However, they snap up any houses that become vacant in Burano and hurry back if they can. It is true that there has been some illegal building but that has not made much difference to the problem. The population used to be in the region of seven or eight thousand, now we are barely six thousand. When someone goes away a whole family is broken up. Something should be done to help these people find proper housing here. We cannot manage this on our own resources. Because, if too many people go away Burano will die. Yes, it is now a lively place, particularly in the summer when there are so many tourists about. Every morning in the season six or seven hundred of them disembark here, mostly from the tourist launches, not from the *vaporetti, ma però* they only stay for twenty minutes. They do not see anything, they do not get to understand anything. The lace school no longer exists. It was a disaster when it was closed three years ago.

Apart from tourism the only other jobs are in fishing or the glassworks in Murano. A great many people work in Murano. As for fishing, those who have been able to afford to build new boats, properly equipped for trawling out in the open sea, live pretty well. Yes, there are still a lot of young men fishing but they are men who have inherited the boat and equipment. If all the family money is wrapped up in the boat and gear you might say that they *had* to become fishermen. They *have* to follow in their fathers' footsteps. The only other possible employment here is in the little canning factory which puts up fish in tins, but it is only busy for two or three months at the most in the year.

Now Burano has tidied itself up. It is clean and sanitary

and nearly everyone owns his own house. The people are not rich but they are not as poor as they used to be and to them cleanliness is everything. They now expect — and can pay for — some comfort in their lives and are constantly improving their living conditions. Cleanliness is the key. They would rather eat less and have a clean, well-cared for house. This is their real passion. They want everyone who passes the door to notice how spick and span the interior is. Their pride is in the house, not in their cars like a lot of people on the *terraferma*. Some do have cars because they need them for their work. I do not have a car, for instance. I have a boat, of course, but a car is no use to me in my business. It is mostly the shopkeepers who need cars to transport the stock they need. There are maybe a hundred people with cars here in Burano out of six thousand. I should be very surprised if there were more. The rest of us may need to go to Treporti, to the *terraferma* once a week or so. So it would not be worth our while to own a car just for pleasure, a sort of whim or luxury.

Young people seem reasonably content here. You can tell that from the fact that very few go away even during the summer holidays. At the most they go over to the beach at Treporti and that, after all, is the nearest beach. There is dancing and other amusements over there. There is nothing here except the cinema. We have two cinemas. Mostly the young people get hold of a boat and go off fishing with their friends. The young people, like their elders, mostly work in Murano but a lot of the school-leavers, the boys that is to say, become fishermen for a time, till they have found something else or while they are waiting for their call-up for military service. The young men who stick to fishing are mostly the trawlermen these days, who fish in the Adriatic. Our trawlers do not usually go a long way out to sea. Our boats are not made for long trips on the high seas and they seldom go more than two or three miles from the coast.

We get our supplies of fish either from local fishermen or from our wholesaler, who is my cousin as it happens. From the fishermen we get the lagoon specialities such as sole, eel, *passerini*, *calamari*, *seppioline*, the tastier lagoon fish in fact. Our lagoon sole, for instance, is very good, particularly the

110

ones we call *la paurose,* and *la gentile* which is the best of all. For the other fish we need I telephone my orders overnight for things like *scampi* which now mostly come up from Sicily or from Yugoslavia or over towards Trieste. We don't get *scampi* locally. You have to go out to sea for them. Our own *scampi,* that is to say Italian *scampi,* are mostly from Sicily. Of course you can get frozen *scampi* from all sorts of places — but not in this restaurant, you don't. Nothing frozen here! Every single thing fresh, fresh every day. You might say that fresh fish is our trade mark. Our reputation has been built on the freshness of our fish. Naturally we have refrigerators but these are to keep our supplies in perfect condition, and our supplies come in every morning, every morning. Our suppliers bring us every day seven or eight different kinds of fish depending on the season and what is the best of the catch that day.

Me get up early? On the contrary, I get up very late but then I stay up very late too. I do all the ordering late in the evening and my cousins buy everything I need and send it along next morning or the fishermen come in to show us their catch and sell direct. It is *la mamma* who checks everything in. She is really the key to the whole operation. She has an extensive knowledge of fish and can tell at a glance whether it is of first quality or not.

We do not have much free time in this business. When I am free I usually stay in Italy. Next to Burano I love Italy. I want to get to know Italy really well before I start going to other countries. Recently I have been in Sicily. Once I did go to Switzerland for a few days. In this business one makes a lot of friends and I have invitations to go to France and Germany and other places. But I don't know when I shall be able to go. I seldom go away for more than three or four days at a time. I like being at home, you see. And then if you are going to run a business properly you have to be around. As we say, *"L'occhio del padrone ingrassa la vacca"* (the master's eye fattens the cow). You have to know just how and when to notice things. I am very fortunate, I have help in whom I have as much confidence as I have in myself, as I said just now. They know that if I am not around they have full responsibility just as though they were me. I think it is rare to find such a relationship these days but this is the way it is here and we like it this way.

Compared with the old days things are not too bad in Burano. Apart from owning their houses the men bring in good wages today. In the old days health here in the island was one of the great worries. There used to be recurring out-breaks of typhus mostly from eating bad shellfish. People did not know how to keep them in those days — but that was a widespread danger. There was a good deal of ill-health owing to housing conditions — mostly over-crowding and humidity. But luckily those difficulties have practically disappeared. The independent artisans — people like fishermen — are also better off and better equipped. Now they all have outboard motors even on the lightest *sandalo*. Before that they had to row out to the fishing grounds. Now they, like everyone else, have a more serene, a more secure life. In a sense they have never really lacked the essentials of life. There is always food in the lagoon if you fish for it. Even today there are some families who just can't manage but that is because they do not know how to manage. It is a simple, healthy life here in general — simple and healthy. We do not have any *signori* (gentry) nor any paupers. We are all of us of much the same kind and much the same level financially and in every other way. So there is not much discord amongst us.

The war was not too bad here either. Food was rather short. We got a bomb once. A plane was going over one night and must have seen some lights and let off a bomb. It killed eleven people. This was a fortified zone. We had German troops garrisoning the fort here, the one just on the left as you turn out of the Mazzorbo canal towards Torcello. It is all overgrown now but it used to be quite an impressive military post. Some of the soldiers used to come here to eat, they became almost part of the family. We had no difficulties with them at all. They were well-behaved, very lonely far away from their families. I have never had any news of any of those people. I would like to know how they got on, whether they got home alive. I would really like to know. They had to leave in a hurry. We were very much struck by that. It was rather frightening. But apart from this we had a

112

pretty quiet war.

The one thing we really lack here now is the lace school. What we need is work for those who know how to make the famous *punto buranello*. Those who know are old and becoming fewer. There should be some way for them to hand on their knowledge to the little girls. The tradition must not be lost. This, not only for Burano but for Italy and the world. This is the only place in the world where this kind of lace is made. And then the school was such a pleasure to visit, it was so interesting to see how the skills were being handed on: to see all those little girls busily stitching away, and all the trained women each working at their special stitch, and the work growing and filling out as it passed from hand to hand. It took five or six trained hands to complete a piece, you know. There are perhaps ten or fifteen women still making lace and they should be handing on their skills. There are still small girls who want to learn. I don't know whether they could make a living but the point is that lace-making is an institution, a part of our life here in Burano, and it is on the point of disappearing. Lace-making to my way of thinking is like painting a picture, making a piece of sculpture or any other work of art. I think that if they could be sure of making a living girls would want to learn the craft. But certainly the old lace-makers should be teaching in a school as well as doing the work that has been commissioned. The government should do something about it. Lace-making is important to tourism in Burano. When the school existed nearly every tourist went there and they were all fascinated watching this ancient art. Now the tourist arrives in these great launches and twenty minutes later . . . *tac, via!* . . . off he goes again. He may snatch a drink or a cup of tea. He walks through the *piazza* and goes away and is not given a chance to understand a thing: *niente, niente*. Sometimes guides come with a party and you see them grouped outside while the guide explains who we are and that we have a collection of paintings, but they do not even put their noses in the door to have a quick look. It is not their custom we are interested in, don't think that is why I get so annoyed. We do not run a bar service here, we are a restaurant and most tourists simply do not have time to have a meal. No, what annoys me is that they are not given enough time to have a proper look round the island. Tourism has become a matter of pressures, of hurry, of scramble. People do not come to Burano for the day, or even for half a day. They come for twenty minutes, or between two *vaporetti*, for a quick bite and off to the next sight. They rush off to Torcello or back to Venice. They don't see Burano. They do not give themselves time to stroll round the *calli*, to wander along the canals, to take things in, to watch the painters working or, in the old days, to wait until the lace school opened after lunch to see lace being made. It would be enough if they had an hour. But twenty minutes! Useless!

Finally I should tell you that Romano's has always been connected with rowing and racing here in Burano. The first group which was formed called itself the Compagnia della Baracola, which is our name for the fish you call ray. This was a sort of support group for the champion rowers of the club. It had sixty or a hundred members and between 1946 and 1952 the club rowers won six first prizes. Then there was a slackening of interest until Strighetta, as we call him, though his proper name is Albino dei Rossi, and Giapate and some others took over. The 1974 regatta will probably be

Strighetta's last racing regatta. He must be fifty-six, I think. He. is still in great form, a tremendously skilful, strong rower, and even this year came fourth in the Historic Regatta in Venice. He has won many, many first prizes. A remarkable record, particularly if you bear in mind that the war interrupted his racing career. He was not able to row for the whole duration of the war and did no racing at all. So it is all the more remarkable that he has done so well.'

A Gondolier

Albino dei Rossi, usually known as Strighetta (little witch), is a well set up man nudging sixty. His proudest boast is that he is a Buranello and, as a respected member of the community, keeps within the demands of its society. He is perhaps the best known citizen of Burano as he has on fourteen occasions carried off the championship of the Venice Historic Regatta. Though he will talk willingly about his rowing career he is essentially modest about it. He is pleased at his success but has worked hard to attain it, just as he has worked hard to attain to the modest comfort which he now enjoys. This is what he had to say about his life in Burano and his racing:

'Everywhere in Burano you will find noise . . . enormous noise. The fishermen go into a bar and have a glass of wine, they talk and it gets louder and louder. They keep one another company and talk and so on. We are like that in Burano.

I began as a fisherman. I was very little, only eight when my *papa* first took me fishing. I did two years school and then went out into the lagoon fishing with my *papa.* I always did the rowing, right from the age of eight. We always had a lot of good food to eat — fish and polenta, fish and polenta — we ate it together, just as we do today. We did not have soup and so on, only good fresh fish, *pero* it was good, very good. And polenta with it. And so I went fishing and learnt to row, always rowing, every day rowing.

At the age of fourteen I started to race quite seriously. I had been rowing for pleasure since I was ten on these light racing gondolas. And I had come in first in a junior race and by the time I was fifteen I was already on the way to being a champion, half-way, you might way, as I was rowing against boys of eighteen and nineteen. By the time I was seventeen, that would be in 1937, I had some hopes of coming in first, one always has hopes, you know. But I was rowing against champions of long experience, real champions they were in those days. I came in fifth. It wasn't bad for an inexperienced boy. That was my first big regatta — the Murano regatta. Actually I was leading and I should have come in first if I had not mistaken the course. With a bit of experience I would not have been so silly. In 1938, when I was eighteen, I came in first in the singles — just one man in the gondola, you understand. From then till 1968 I rowed every year, sometimes I came first, sometimes I came second, except of course, for the war years. I was called up in 1940, in March, and the war started in June. In 1939 I rowed for the first time in the Historic Regatta in Venice and I came first. Up till then I had always rowed in singles. The Historic Regatta is rowed in doubles, in a bigger gondola. This Regatta was suspended during the war. I did not row at all for the whole of '40, '41, '42, '43, '44 and '45 — in fact the best years of a rower's life. I lost the years from nineteen to twenty-five. I rowed again in the great Regatta in 1946; then I came in second, yes, it is quite true, after not rowing for all those years. So, in '39 I was first; '47, first; '48, first; '49, first; '50, first; '51, first; '52, first; six in a row. Then in '53, third. As I said the Historic Regatta is for doubles and my partner had not been well for some time. Then in '54, first again with a new partner. In '55 we were second and then from '56 to '68 first every year. Fourteen firsts in all in the Historic Regatta and in 1968 I was forty-nine years old. Yes, I am very healthy. Here in Burano the air is damp. One eats well and one sleeps well. Yes, I drink a bit, too. All gondoliers do. You talk and you drink a little with your friends. I used not to drink anything at all but during twenty-six years as a gondolier I learnt to drink a bit: it became a habit. I am still a gondolier, Oh, no, the job's not finished yet! I can always be found at the Dogana Traghetto.

I am a Buranello, born here, just round the corner in the via Pizzo in the Terranova. Now I live in the via Giudecca, yes, we have a Giudecca here, just like Venice. We also have a Fondamenta dei Assassini. It is called that because there is a bridge there which used to be called the Ponte della Coppa (the contest), there were many fights there. They were cut-throats mostly and so the quay was called after them. Then there is the Jews' bridge. There were never many Jews here in the old days, but there were always some which is why we had a Giudecca. Then there is the Terranova Bridge which leads over to the part of Burano which was reclaimed from the sea after the rest of Burano had been built. That is why we called it the Isola Nova or Terranova.

I have been a gondolier since 1946. When I was small I was a fisherman and I went on fishing until the war started. Then I had six years as a soldier and now thirty years as a gondolier. Yes, that is right, I came back from the war in 1945 and got my licence as a gondolier very soon. All gondoliers have to be licensed by the Venetian Municipality. I got mine in 1948. They let me have it so soon because of my record as a rower and also because I had been a fisherman. So I was supposed to know about boats. Each gondola has a number like a taxi and a licence. It normally takes at least ten years to enter the Servizio dei Gondolieri. You do not start as a gondolier, but as a *uom* (a man, an assistant). The old *padroni,* that is to say the old gondoliers, each have a *uom,* a younger man as his assistant. But the number, the licence and also the gondola belong to the old *padrone.* Usually you have to remain as an assistant, an apprentice if you like, for ten to twelve years before you can get your own licence. Of course they are all very expert boatmen. Just imagine serving for ten to twelve years as an assistant when you were an ex-pert boatman before you ever started. They are really very highly skilled men, really professional. *Sono bravi.*

I have three sons who are gondoliers. Eh! Sure! The eldest will get his licence this year, I should think. He is thirty and has been an assistant for twelve years. My second son has been an assistant for four years and the youngest only three. So they have some way to go.

A gondolier earns quite well but it is a very short season and he has to work very hard indeed during those months to make enough to live on for the whole year. He has just five

117

months to make a living. Many of them become fishermen for the other months and even labourers during the winter if they have to make ends meet. A gondolier has a good many expenses. He has to eat away from home for one thing. Every day he eats out and it comes expensive. It costs about ten thousand lire a day, you know, to eat out. Ours is not like some trades where you can go home and your wife has cooked you a meal. During our five months' work we start at eight in the morning and we go on till midnight — that means all your meals out. And you need to drink, too. It is hard and thirsty work and you are out in the sun all day. That is why, as I was telling you, I learnt to drink wine. I never drank any before, but in this game you have to. You need it.

Nowadays I leave Burano by the eight o'clock *vaporetto* and I get home at 1.15 at night, every day during the season. I get up at 7.20 and I wash and dress and go for the *vaporetto*. When I get home I wash and have a bite to eat before I go to bed at about two o'clock. I get five hours' sleep during the season, never more. During the season life is *proprio orribile* (pretty dreadful). But as you see, it suits me. I am in very good health and, physically, I am very strong. A lot of my colleagues cannot stand up to the work. It is getting more difficult every day, chiefly because of the *moto ondoso* (the wash created by motor boats). You may have five or six people on board a gondola which is a very delicate boat reacting to every slight movement, very sensitive. To keep it steady and going forward is tricky and heavy work. In the five months of the season we earn about four million lire. We earn it by hard work and it has to last the whole year.

I belong to the *traghetto* (a gondola station which traditionally runs a ferry across the Grand Canal) called the Dogana, opposite the Customs House. It is the first *traghetto* in the Grand Canal. We no longer run a ferry across the Canal because the water is too rough. It used to be the longest ferry, about 200 metres from Harry's Bar to the Customs. At times we had as many as twelve or thirteen people standing in these big boats. They get frightened when it begins to bounce about and so we had to stop the ferry service. We stopped it four years ago.

The *traghetti* are very old. There have been ferry services across the Grand Canal for centuries. It was the duty of each gondola station to run a *traghetto* but some of them are now out of service. There was the Dogana (now suspended), Santa Maria del Giglio, S. Tomà, S. Benetto, Carbon (now suspended), Santa Sofia or the Cà' d'Oro, S. Marcuola (now suspended), and the Railway Station (now suspended).

There are 389 gondoliers at present. The Danieli station has about 46 gondoliers; S. Marco, 60; Dogana, 30; Bauer, 40; Santa Maria del Giglio, 28; S. Tomà, 26 or 27; S. Benetto, 40; Carbon 38; Santa Sofia, 28 or 29; S. Felice, 12; Marcuola, 14; Station, 80.

The Venetians still use the gondolas, *certo!* Only the *traghetti, però!* They do not hire gondolas. It is not like the old days. But many Italians from other cities hire them. Florentines, Romans, Neopolitans, Milanese all hire gondolas. They are nice people, *bravi,* and generous too. They always pay well, the Italians, and they are courteous, too. They come to Venice to ride in a gondola and those who ride in a gondola are prepared to pay for the pleasure. Nice people! In the old days the Venetians used to take a gondola to go to the opera at the Fenice theatre, but never nowadays. They walk or maybe they take a *vaporetto,* or if they are in a hurry to catch a train or have a lot of luggage they take a motor-boat. There are no more private gondolas either. Every palace, every big house, used to have its gondola with its neat *felze* (a cabin built amidships) and its gondoliers in livery. Now the Venetians prefer a motor-boat.

I usually start the season on March 15; that is to say that from that date I am always at the *traghetto* near Harry's Bar, and I am there every day until November. Then I do not go any more. There is really no custom during the winter.

Things have greatly changed in recent years, even in an old trade like ours. There used to be a close organisation of gondoliers, a real sort of co-operative. If one of us died the others looked after the widow and children and saw that they were brought up properly and taught a trade. There were feasts and festivities and we were really like a family, like brothers. But all this has disappeared. Now, of course, if some disaster overtakes a family we all contribute some-

119

thing, send flowers to the funeral and that is all. I suppose we think now that it is for the state to help people who are in trouble these days. The young do not look after the old any more either. There is a kind of lack of respect, of self-respect too. You see it amongst our clients. People are becoming nasty, I mean the people who take our boats. We have rich people, English, Americans, Japanese now too, people from all over the world, and a motor-boat dashes by and everybody gets soaked. As I said, it is very difficult to control a gondola in a choppy sea especially when fully loaded with five or six people. Of course our clients get cross when dirty canal water is slopped over their fine clothes — and they go for us. It is not our fault. We have been using all our skill but you can't always help it when water splashes aboard. Visitors to Venice ride in a gondola because they want to be quiet and have a little peace and not be tossed about by waves and splashed by dirty water. It is difficult now in all the canals. People think that there is choppy water only in the Grand Canal, but this is not true. Actually there is more heavy traffic in the little canals. There are barges going to and fro supplying hotels and cafés, loaded down with bottles, there are *mototopi* carrying all sorts of freight chugging along, creating a great wash which can bash a gondola up against a wall, and so on. I really do not see any solution. People have to work, bricks must be delivered to building sites, food, drink, goods must be ferried about and the canals are the only way to do it. I know that some people say that some of the canals should be closed at certain times to allow peace and quiet for the tourists riding in gondolas. But all these canals serve houses and businesses and they must live. You cannot close any canals to business traffic. Things are going badly for us gondoliers in Venice, this is true. For us who are fifty or more, it was fairly easy to be a gondolier. For the young ones it is very difficult. My sons are going to find it much more difficult than I did. The work is heavier — you cannot imagine what hard work it is controlling a heavily laden gondola in the cross wash of motor-boats. It looks easy because rowing our way is a question of weight and balance, but it also requires muscle, you know, and judgment. Then every year there are more transport boats and motor-boats and even if they keep strictly to the speed limits, and they mostly do, there is not time between one *mototopo* passing and the next for the water to return to a reasonable calm. For example in the last four years the *moto ondoso* has doubled in effect — in just four years. If the *moto ondoso* goes on increasing at this rate it will not be possible to row at all in these waters and the gondola will disappear. I know and I am telling you true. Soon it will only be possible to work from eight or nine in the evening until about eleven and then knock off. In the daytime it is already practically impossible to work with a light, fragile boat like a gondola. Then, the young gondoliers lose their tempers when they get swamped by a passing boat — after all they are working just as much as the driver of a big *mototopo* or a motor-boat. But it does not do any good to yell and curse and damn the other chap. The young ones really do not have much respect. When they cannot bear it any more they go off and get a job in a glass factory. After all that long apprenticeship it seems a waste. It is a good trade being a gondolier, and interesting and very skilled, but you can't blame men for leaving it if the conditions of work are impossible. In fact, in Venice the *moto ondoso* is a big problem. I think the gondola will disappear.

A new working gondola, all fitted out, usually costs about three million two hundred or three hundred lire. A year's pay more or less, but what are you going to eat during the year and how are you going to pay the rent and clothe your children? Eh? We have two co-operatives about equal in membership which help us to buy and replace our gondolas. When a gondolier needs a new one, he goes to the president, who is, of course, one of us, a gondolier himself who understands the craft, or the the vice-president, and gets a loan. Besides this, each gondola station has a *capo* (chief). We call him a *gastaldo* and he is always chosen by the gondoliers working at that station. There are four *capi* in each station and the office usually goes the round. I have never been a *gastaldo*. I would rather not be in office. I just want to be a gondolier. That is all I want: to row my gondola. I just want to be Strighetta *è basta* (and that's all).

I became known as Strighetta a long time ago. I was born

here in Burano and my *papa* was too, and my *papa's papa* and so on. Long ago, there were no lights in the streets of Burano. Street lighting is quite recent here. Before that we had tiny *ferraretti* (little oil burners) at some street corners, which gave a glimmer of light every so often in the dark *calli*. Only the lace-ladies, you know the women who made the lace, used to go about among the houses after dark. Everybody else and especially all the young people were always safe home after dark, which was usually at about half-past eight. *E ciò, per forza*, it was a scandal for young people to be out after dark. Some of my cousins used to go off and see their girl friends and when they came out they ran into these old women who were on their way home and the old women used to say: "And what are you doing out at this time of night? The *strighe* (witches) will get you!" These young relatives of mine believed all this. Because I was out at all hours calling on my girl friend and did not seem to come to any harm they began to say that it was because I was a little witch myself and they started calling me Strighetta which means little witch, and somehow the name stuck. We all have nicknames in Burano, maybe to avoid confusion because so many of us have the same names.

Nowadays young people are out till after midnight and nobody thinks anything of it. But when I was young the whole island was closed up at dusk with everybody indoors except those old women and the boys who had girl friends and were not afraid of witches!

The Burano rowing club headquarters is Romano's restaurant, as you know. If you go there you will see, in the showcase with the name of the club, La Baracola we called it, after the name of the fish, all the pennants we have won at the Venice Historic Regatta and also two certificates, one for my friend and partner Giapate (Giapate means someone who grabs things, a grabber, if you like, though I don't think he has ever grabbed anything, he is too gentle and courteous — Marcello Bon is his real name). We were awarded these certificates when we won our fifth championship. Giapate is not too well these days and cannot work any more. He is two years older than me. He was born in 1918 and I was born in 1920. Ciaci is also a great champion. His real name is

Tagliapietra but he is always called Ciaci. He is a champion racer, *un campione forte, madonna.* He has rowed in Australia and also in Tokyo. He does not live here. He lives in Pellestrina. He is really *un campione forte, fuori classe.*

It is true that rowing is a gift but you have to think about it too. I started rowing when I was small. After two years I left school, as I told you, and went fishing with my father. I soon noticed that the less movement you made the faster the boat went. You had to be quiet and stable and in balance and I practised and improved and I found that even a millimetre of

movement could affect the behaviour of the boat. At ten years old I was already rowing pretty well, even better at twelve. Then I joined the rowing club of the Acquirini. I have always rowed *alla veneziana* as we say, that is standing up and facing the front but with only one oar, not like the men you see rowing *sandali* with two oars. I stayed for four years with that club, rowing in these very small boats. I learnt that it was easier to row in the larger boats because they were more stable. It was also an advantage to me that I was developing well physically because rowing *alla veneziana* or *alla valesana* is to some extent a question of weight. A lot depends on how you throw your weight on the oar. The boat reacts to every slight movement. The smaller the boat the more sensitive it is. I learnt to row on a small boat and I became a champion. In Venice they tried hard to alter my style but I would not change. Before the war in Venice they rowed in a quite different way from me, I had learnt and practised on much smaller boats, like the *gondolini* that are used in the Historic Regatta.

These *gondolini* belong to the Venetian Municipality. No. 1 is white, 2 is yellow, 3 is violet, 4 is blue, 5 is red, 6 is green, 7 is orange, 8 is pink, 9 is brown, 10 is black. These *gondolini* are much lighter than the boats used in the Burano regatta.

Giapate and I were partners in a *gondolino*. You should never change partners if you can avoid it. Once you get to know your partner and his manner of rowing you should stick together if you want to succeed: like Ciaci and his partner Fonghe, that is to say Giuseppe, or like Giapate and me.

The Voga Longa is a big thing. So many people have become interested in rowing that hundreds of them joined in. Rowing is good for you, you know. It is wonderful exercise and you have to train, for at least two months, if you want to take part in the Voga Longa. It is a thirty kilometre race. It starts at nine in the morning and some do not get back till six at night. It starts at S. Marco, goes to S. Erasmo, Burano, Mazzorbo, Murano, Canareggio and down the Grand Canal back to S. Marco. There must be at least 600 boats taking part. They are not all champions but they all get home. Between nine in the morning and six in the evening there are nine hours and thirty kilometres to do so it is not a terrible speed. Even if you only go at four kilometres an hour, very soft and slow, you will get home. Even you could do that! You row nice and slow and then eat a bit and on you go. I raced in the Voga Longa last year. It was the first year the race had ever been held. It was fun and a great success. In future it should be even better because there will be more boats. The race starts in the Basin of S. Marco and all the traffic is stopped (they stopped the traffic at eight o'clock)

124

and the water is calm with hardly a ripple. Wonderful water for rowing, water you hardly ever see these days. then, off you all go! Terrific!'

A Wood Carver

Not all the Venetian traditional crafts flourish equally. We have seen the prosperity in recent times of the glass-blowing trade and the dwindling of lace-making. Wood-carving is another craft in decline in spite of a long tradition of its use in church and secular ornament and in furniture. There are several wood carvers in Burano but only one who manages to make a living. The wood carver who talked to me is not the lucky one. He is an excellent craftsman and a sensitive painter forced into a job of no interest to him to provide for his family. Yet he is not a frustrated man but uses his intelligence and goodwill in an attempt to advance the society in which he lives. This is what he said:

'It is certain that Burano is not a society that hankers after a cultural life, in the sense that the people feel the need of the arts as a way of living a fuller life. But we live in a setting of great poetry, of extraordinary historical and natural beauty, and I think this affects them whether they recognise it or not.

Burano is chiefly noted in the world of painting because of the work of the Burano school of painters. I am thinking of the nineteenth century and of men like Gino Rossi, Pier Semmeghini and the others who came later and who made Burano their base.

The people of Burano are interested in the exhibitions and so on which are mounted every year but these exhibitions never give rise to any discussions and there never develops from them (and this is what is really lacking) any desire to take things further, to analyse, to ask what are the motives, the "why?" of art. The arts should be a crucial point in the cultural life of the mass of people, of the cultural development both of the individual and of society. No? What I am trying to say is that cultural activities here always remain on the surface, at the superficial level. For instance, young people here do quite a lot of painting. Why? Because every

125

year there is an exhibition called the Premio Burano (the Burano Award) which distributes prizes, big prizes, little prizes, consolation prizes to pretty nearly everyone with the slightest competence. Now, art is not like this. It demands sacrifices, thought and persistence. It requires practically all that an individual has to give. It needs a continual, dedicated, loving search to identify and to clarify what one wants to do and then to find a way of doing it and reaching one's highest standard. You cannot blame any Buranelli who do not do this. What is wrong is that cultural matters do not receive that serious consideration of aims and methods which will enable them to reach, to make a difference to, a community or an individual. You must offer him your hand. You must not force him to put out his hand. And if you do it properly you will have done much more than opening cultural horizons. You will give him standards which will make him a more co-operative and clear-minded member of a self-governing society.

Here in Burano we have no guidance, no encouragement, no help from the Ministries of Cultural Affairs or of Public Instruction, or from the regional government or from the municipality of Venice. There is a section of the Università Popolare which has for a long time organised cultural activities. But here we have noticed that there is a growing tendency to stress immediate preoccupations and problems, which are often very interesting but which do not get to the root of cultural development. For instance, there was a series of excellent and highly successful lectures on sexual education. They drew large audiences including women and young people who not only listened but asked questions and took a real part in discussions. Health education was another very popular subject. The stress, as you see, was on some specific subject of direct concern. The lectures did stir up a great deal of interest even if it was of a kind that you might describe as self-centred or materialistic and even if it was sometimes tinged with a rather morbid kind of curiosity arising from the breaking of old taboos on the discussion of certain subjects. More helpful in creating a cultural environment and giving us information about ourselves and our environment and our past were the lectures organised earlier

126

by the Università Popolare on such themes as the local history of Burano, on the Venetian painters, on Venetian and Burano gastronomy, the theatre of Goldoni and so on.

More could be done on the basis of our dialect. We all speak it among ourselves. So do the young people. Dialect does not seem to be giving way to Italian, at least not in Burano. But social pressure is partly responsible for this. If anyone starts talking Italian he is immediately accused of giving himself airs. Our dialect is very important to us and we recognise it as a vehicle of our personality which distinguishes us from other Italians. But the authorities don't use this for any constructive purpose. No attempt is made to relate our language to our history or our surroundings or any of these to national history or culture. The schools, for instance, talk about Garibaldi and Cavour and so on but they don't talk about us at that time or what we thought and did about it all, or teach us about our background, and the flora and fauna which surround us. Television does not help us either because it only deals with national issues and never with the aspects of life which touch us most nearly.

We have a library. It is organised by the centre for permanent education. It is housed in the elementary school and keeps school holidays. This means that it is shut for four months in the year. It is only open in the afternoons when most people are at work. It is a small collection and it cannot cater to any wide range of interests. It does not have the impact that it should have and for the same reasons as before, that is to say the neglect of proper methods of encouraging people. The Buranelli would certainly respond to a lead. Many of them do read but they dither about, not knowing how to read or what to read or where to find things that interest them, so they take the line of least resistance and read what everybody else reads, romances, strip cartoons and funnies. But given a chance how they do respond!

About five years ago some of us living here in Burano organised a little experiment in co-operation with the headmaster of the school, who was very open-minded and well aware of the problems of Italian education. Our little group worked out a different approach to the *doposcuola*, which is what they call the voluntary activities which take place in schools during term-time after school hours. We offered the children in the fourth and fifth classes of the primary level a selection of courses to which they could come if they wanted, or not just as they pleased. We found people with competence in French and music and physical education. I offered to teach art. The results achieved by this little experiment were beyond all our hopes. We were astonished and delighted. The boys and girls poured in from this quite small community. To talk only of my own experience: I taught for five months between Christmas and May, and at the start of my course I had ten children who came for one session a week. At the end of the period I was giving several sessions a week to some thirty to thirty-five youngsters. Children came who had always regarded the *doposcuola* as a bore and a waste of time. With us they worked hard and were really beginning to develop a sense of colour and a feeling for light and shade in a composition. The other members of the group had a similar experience and we were looking forward to carrying on in the next year with an activity which apart from giving us great satisfaction seemed to be making a modest contribution to the education of the children of our island. And — would you believe it — we were not allowed to go on. A combination of bureaucracy and a trade union boycott ("Who are those people teaching in the *doposcuola*? They are not teachers. They are usurping our privileges.") killed off our experiment, and put something routine and rule of thumb in its place.

Until I was twenty-three years old I was a sculptor in wood. I still carve when I can find the time but unfortunately this is not very often as my job is demanding, time-consuming and infinitely sterile. I would gladly change it but it is difficult to change horses in mid-stream. Life is uncertain in any of the arts and in 1953 I found myself without a job. At that time I had the opportunity to take over a grocer's shop and, although it was not my notion of a congenial life, it has at least given my wife and myself security, and the possibility of launching our family, and this house. That is a satisfaction. It would be a greater satisfaction to live in — or better still to help build — a society where each could give the best of himself to the community and not one where, when the people get into the wrong box, society shrugs its shoulders and says *"S'arrangia lui, poverino"* ("It's up to him to cope, poor lad").

My father was the sort of man who would have been able to cope. He was a good merchant, energetic, hard-working and with excellent judgment. In his business he sold everything, boots, shoes, trousers, shirts, everything for the house except food. His was the only business of its kind and he travelled over a wide area of the Veneto, buying, selling, exchanging. He used to cover Treporti, Cavallino, Jesolo, Latisano, Grado, Portogruaro, as well as Burano and S. Erasmo nearer to Venice. He used to go off for weeks at a time and say to my mother, "Well, my dear, I shall not see you again until I have bought a house." He put all his savings into houses. In 1931 or 1932 he bought the house we lived in here in Burano. It is a beautiful house in the *piazza* here and he always said he earned it in one season. It cost him 22,000 lire at that time. In those days if you had ten houses you could live comfortably on the rents.

After the war houses were no longer an attractive investment, partly because the lire had gone down in value and house prices and gone up to match, and partly because rents were controlled and tenants given security of tenure. All this coincided with wages going up. The price of fish went up too and the fishermen were becoming capitalists. There was no longer any question of poor fisherfolk. So just at a time when the house-owners were beginning to think their houses a burden and an expense and tenants who complained to the rent tribunals a nuisance, and were considering selling off, the people of Burano had enough money to buy them up. Within a fairly short time 87 per cent of the Burano families owned their own house. A change for the better. A great step forward.'

An Official

If officials must be nameless and faceless they should not be thought to be without personality or interest in the community they serve. This is what one of them had to say:

'My father was a skipper-steersman in the *vaporetto* service. We were a large family. There were ten of us at home, my father, mother and eight of us children.

I did my elementary schooling here during the war and finished the five years. In those days you had to go in to Venice to continue with the secondary level, and I did the first three years before I had to give up. It was partly my fault that I gave up and partly family circumstances. I must have been about twelve when I started secondary school. I used to leave home at seven in the morning and usually only got home at seven at night, and I used to take a lunch box with me. It was a long day for a boy of that age. With only one wage-earner in a family of that size you can imagine that things were not very easy. Providing the essential school books was hard enough and more than that was just not possible. So, I never had an encyclopaedia, I had never seen a dictionary. My parents did all they possibly could to give us a proper education. But the atmosphere was against being properly educated. Most of my friends were the sons of fishermen and other craftsmen who needed the boys to help them as soon as possible, and once the day's work was over they wanted to go off amusing themselves. Any free time I had was taken up with homework which was difficult anyway in a small crowded house. My friends used to say: "Come on with us. Let us take the boat and go fishing," and I used to allow myself to be tempted. Yes, I let myself be led astray, *ecco!*

But you must not think that I do not believe in schooling. I certainly do but perhaps in a different sort of schooling. I would like to see more stress laid on human values. It really does not seem to me to matter what facts you know, whether you know who Garibaldi or Galileo or Shakespeare was or what is the theorem of Pythagoras. I think that schooling should prepare children to appreciate cultural things and attain them for themselves. This is what I think. I do not have this and I have not won it for myself because I threw away my opportunity of being educated and then later on I got married and had a family of my own and became a municipal officer with, it is true, some responsibility. Then there is the difficulty of distance. There are no cultural opportunities here in Burano. You have to go to Venice and we are a long way from Venice. I do not mean we are distant in miles. No, but we are distant in time. You have to reckon on half a day to get an hour's reading, for instance, in Venice because of the time it takes to get there in a *vaporetto* and then walking across the town.

So little by little I turned my mind more to ways in which I could perhaps help with social activities here in Burano. For instance in 1959 we set up an association here to try to create a civic centre. We were greatly helped by the doctor we had here then, a marvellous man who, besides being a good doctor, helped so many people in trouble — a real Franciscan for kindliness. Dr Bassan his name was. We all loved him and we put up a bronze plaque on his house near the *vaporetto* landing-stage. The association had 300 members and did all sorts of things to improve conditions here in Burano. For instance, it negotiated with A.C.N.I.L., which is the Venetian municipal authority for public transport in the lagoon, to start the service of *motonave*. Until then we only had the *vaporetti* and they were just not big enough to transport all the workers to and from Murano. They used to be absolutely crammed and there were always many of us who had to stand on the open deck, after working with the furnaces all day too. In the winter you got really cold and wet. Certainly I never seemed to get a place inside because I could never get away from my job till the last minute and every winter I went down with bronchitis. Bronchitis and pneumonia, we all got them. In the *motonave* there is room comfortably for everybody in the cabins. You are warm and dry and you can sit down. And in the summer it is better for the tourists, too, who now live over in Jesolo in such large numbers. So the *motonave* service during the rush hours is a great improvement and the civic association helped to get it.

It also organised more cultural things. Tours, for instance, to places of note like Ravenna and Asolo. We ran courses for adults in the arts and languages, mostly English and German and some exhibitions. Then with the creation of the ward councils under the municipality the association fell off a bit. People expected the ward council to take over and lost interest themselves.

Later I was asked to help with the activities of E.N.A.L.

131

(National Association for Workers' Leisure-time Activities) which is chiefly concerned with social and cultural activities. This is a large national association and necessarily rather bureaucratic in its methods but still we managed to do a number of interesting things with the help of E.N.A.L. and of course of the school here too. We ran language courses (French this time) and arranged driving lessons.

When we began hardly anybody here had a car and so did not know how to drive. Now about a hundred of us have cars. For instance I have a car. I started with a second-hand Fiat and when that wore out (it was ten years old) I got an Audi, not a big one. It is very useful for my wife's business. She has a little shop and we go to the warehouses in the car and transport the things she needs ourselves. It is really necessary to have some quick, reliable transport. It costs so much these days to send things by the *mototopi* carriers and takes such a long time. So instead of waiting for deliveries we fetch the things in the car and bring them over bit by bit from Treporti in the *vaporetto*. Yesterday we went to a warehouse in Treviso. At other times we go to Padua or Mestre and so on, depending on what my wife needs to buy. We use the car for pleasure too. We have driven all over the Dolomites and in Austria and Yugoslavia.

So, to go back to what I was saying, we organise exhibitions and day trips and little tours. We have been to Belluno up in the mountains and Pordenone and Portogruaro. All over the Veneto in fact, and naturally also to Venice. At first our tours only numbered four or five but people enjoyed them and they gradually increased up to twenty people. But now this activity is tailing off too. People are very ready to join in and really enjoy themselves but there is a lot of hard work involved and not many want to help with that.

What I would really like to do now is to find some way of helping people who suffer, whatever the reason, whether it is an individual who needs help or a community hit by some calamity. There should be a fund in the hands of some recognised competent organisation like the Red Cross which could intervene immediately in case of need. I spend most of my time now trying to work out a scheme and, I am glad to say,

132

the Italian Red Cross seems interested. That is very encouraging.

We could have done with some help of this kind in 1966 during the great flood of November 4. Fortunately nobody in Burano lost their lives but an enormous amount of damage was done. I thought we might be in trouble when I saw how fast the water was rising, fast that is to say compared with the usual rate of flow of the tide. I thought, *mamma mia!* The *scirocco* was blowing very hard. The *palude* were already covered and this meant that the rising tide was coming straight at us without any obstacle at all. It came straight from the sea! We very soon realised the danger. We had no means of knowing how much the water would rise or where it would stop. We knew, of course, that the water rises and falls alternately for six hours. But when we saw that it went on rising after the normal six hours of rising tide we said to ourselves, *"Ma, come mai?* What is going on now? How long will the water continue to flow in?" And the wind continued to rise. The *scirocco* is the south wind and it seemed to be bringing the whole Adriatic into the lagoon. People had already started shifting their more precious belongings upstairs but, you know our houses, there is not much room and the stairs are narrow, and it is not easy to move things in a hurry. My wife and I moved as much of her stock as we could to the top shelves but, of course, there was not room for everything. Soon the counters were awash. In order to go on working in the shop I had to put on one of those fisherman's garments, you know, rubber boots and overall all in one piece. Mine came right up to my armpits. Rubber thigh-boots were not high enough. They were actually dangerous because the water slopped inside them and upset your balance. You understand? Then someone came along with a boat which we took right into the shop and started loading it with bales of material and dress lengths and all sorts of things and took it along to my house just along the quay. By great good luck I live upstairs — I have an apartment, not a house. As you know, most people in Burano live on the ground floor, that is to say the kitchen and any other living rooms they have are on the ground floor and the bedrooms up above. But the whole of my accommodation is upstairs.

133

We started carrying as much as we could upstairs and stacking it in the rooms. We could not take everything. I don't mind telling you that we lost a lot of stock, things soaked or damaged by salt water because you must remember that it was the sea coming in. We were not insured. Everybody is insured against fire but nobody against floods. Nobody ever dreamt that the *acqua alta* could come so high. Then, a tide rises slowly and everybody reckoned that there would be time to move things, that we would have some warning. After all we do know when the *acqua alta* is likely to happen, depending on the wind and the moon; the tide comes in more strongly when the moon is waxing than when it is waning and we know also that it is more likely to happen between November and March, In fact, we can tell pretty well not only when we will get an *acqua alta* but also about how high it will come. The people of Venice may not know these things. But we Buranelli do. After all, the lagoon is our life and most of us have been fishermen at some time or other in our lives. This does not mean that we are always right. The *acqua alta* is affected by things we know nothing about, for instance a wind out at sea which is not felt here in the lagoon, and we cannot take this sort of thing into account. But taken by and large we know when the *acqua alta* will come and can judge how high it will come. But not in November 1966. We were all caught out. Nobody really had time to take precautions. Some people even had their beds under water, their mattresses soaked, crockery and food floating round in the cupboards. We all had to cope as best as we could because nobody had time, at first, to help anyone else. Towards afternoon people who had done all they could to save their own things began to help their friends and neighbours. The drinking water was polluted, the electric light failed. I remember telephoning to the fire brigade in Mestre to see if we could get some help and it was only then that we discovered how extensive the floods were and what a disaster had hit us all. Everybody was in the same mess. We were without bread for a day in Burano. In Venice they were without for several days.

But I can tell you one thing which was marvellous. The next day when the sun came out Burano was a hive of industry. Here beds were being carried out to dry in the sun, there furniture, clothes, curtains, mattresses were spread out on the quays and *campielli* and *calli* to dry. And do you know, not a thing disappeared, not a thing was pinched. Everybody was busy, sweeping out water, washing down walls, cleaning floors, polishing furniture, washing and ironing clothes and curtains. It was really marvellous to see, I can't describe how marvellous it was. All those people who had been struck by this calamity, who had borne all this, were so happy to have survived as well as they had. They were really contented and happy to have escaped. They were all good-tempered and gay and helpful to one another. Look, I am a local man and I just went round looking at my islanders in admiration. A real pleasure it was to see and I said to myself: 'Well, it just goes to show that in case of real difficulty we still know how to react, how to overcome.' It was marvellous to see, *ecco!* Perhaps all this good humour and cheerfulness was caused by the strain and sadness of the previous day. I suppose everybody felt a sense of relief that it was over and a sense of fellowship in danger. I certainly felt it. I am still a young man and I have seen some danger. All we boys here go out swimming and sailing and while we were not reckless we ran into some dangers as boys do. We Buranelli do not take fright at every little thing. But that flood, well, we knew how dangerous it was. If the water had come up another couple of feet half the houses in Burano would have collapsed. They are old houses, you know, and not very solid. You don't notice that as they are all so pretty and well-cared for. But the sea was very rough and the houses could not have stood up to it. People do not realise, even in Venice, how rough the sea was in the open lagoon. I suppose this sense of solidarity came from the knowledge that there was real danger and that nobody could help us. We were really up against it and alone — just amongst ourselves. When you read of all the violence in the world, done by people who have jobs and houses and enough to eat and all the things you most need, you really begin to think that hard times might be good for us, to bring us all together and give us a sense of solidarity, of human kindness. I don't know, but it does make you think when you see how people

135

behave in a disaster. Do you know, that day in Burano there was not a drunk in sight, nobody cursing and swearing, no tempers, no thieving. Everybody was marvellous!

The government helped with grants to pay for some of the damage to people's property. It did not pay for everything, of course, and there were some who got more than their share. But there are always some crafty ones. That is the way it goes nowadays. For as long as everyone wants to receive and no one wants to give, things will go badly. I may not be a man of great culture or education but that is what I think.'

*

Young People

A Boy of Sixteen

'Burano is a very closed society and is at least ten years behind the times. If you are brought up here you find that you have adopted the Buranelli attitudes and ways of thought and you find you are rather ridiculous when you go elsewhere, for instance to Venice. It is traumatic! You have to change all your ideas in a hurry and you end up doing it all wrong because you do not know what the new society wants you to think. By that time you have forgotten what the Burano people think about things so that you are not comfortable there any more either.

Young people feel that youth has a better profile elsewhere and that is another reason why they want to go away. As soon as they become independent they want to go, particularly those who marry young and want to make their way. We all get fed up with the pressures of this closed society. We want to get out and breathe some air.'

*

A Boy of Seventeen

'For young people there are two difficulties about Burano. There is not much scope and things are a bit static here and distance is probably the cause of both.

For instance, for my training I have to go to Mestre. Last

136

year my day was made up of four hours' travel and five hours' training. I used to leave at six in the morning and get home about half-past three. It was a long day. Now my course is in another building and my travel time is less. If I stay here it will be like this all my life because I am not likely to find a job in my line (I am going to be a surveyor) and I shall have to spend hours every day travelling.

Then one comes home from the world outside to a very old-fashioned, traditional society, satisfied with its hum-drum, repetitive sort of life. The trouble is that it is isolated and new ideas don't circulate. Lots of us feel enclosed in our families. We have different views, different values and want a different life. But it is not only the families. If you look at the town you see that its shape — all these little houses huddled together with water all round — gives a feeling of claustrophobia. You get the impression of being shut up and at the same time terribly isolated, far away from everything that seems important.

Some people here, but not very many, try to do something to improve things here in Burano and do something about this static state of affairs. But it is uphill work. Most of their initiatives get thrown out and that is depressing and they finally give up.

If you want to do anything in life, make the most of your opportunities, you have to leave Burano and go *fuori* (out-side). That is inevitable, even if you have made an effort to change things a bit and even if you go unwillingly. *Certo*, we go unwillingly! If there were any vitality in this community or even any possibility of making changes we would most of us stay. I myself am very likely to go. I should be sorry to leave this beautiful, stupendous setting, but I can do without Burano society as it is now.

It would help, I think, if we had some place of our own where we could meet and discuss things among ourselves. There is a young priest here, he is the assistant to the *monsignore* who is getting on a bit now, who is very helpful and brings us together to discuss things. There is a small group of us who meet fairly regularly to think out various subjects, for instance how a Christian should behave in today's society. It is interesting and helpful. He also takes great trouble with organising *feste*. There was a huge one for St. Francis's Day which was a great success. But what we need is a place of our own, properly organised. There are various places which we can use for various purposes but there are restrictions on them all because they link up with the Church or one of the political parties. We need a centre for young people. This would be good for us and perhaps for Burano, because it might help to shake the people out of their lethargy and make them a little less self-satisfied. That's what it is really, they are self-satisfied and if anyone thinks the least bit differently from themselves they are automatically excluded, they have no chance of participating usefully in the community any more. There are people in the island who would never leave Burano if they were not forced to do so for their work.

There is a sports centre but it seems to be used only by the football club and if you don't happen to play football, it isn't much good to you. It is called the polysport centre but it is really a monosport centre. Otherwise there is the cinema or you make your own activities. Some go out in boats. Some go to Treporti to dance or even to Venice when they have time, but it takes an hour each way. So even if there were any youth activities in Venice we could not really take part. But we are going to have an Olympic swimming pool in Venice! So they say! They have been promising us a swimming pool for a hundred years at least. We will see.'

*

A Boy of Fifteen

'That ridiculous fight about the swimming pool! And even when they have got it, it won't help us here in Burano. They will leave us to go on belly-flopping in the lagoon.'

*

A Girl of Sixteen

'Since I left school I have been helping here in the shop. I enjoy it a lot. People are always coming in and out and you

138

know what is going on. There are lots of things to do here in Burano. I go out in the boat with my friends in the summer, seven or eight of us together in several boats. Yes, I know there are some mothers who don't like their girls going off in boats with boys, but we are not like that, we always stay together and we do not go hiding in the *ghebi*. Then there is the cinema. I go every week with my friends. We go dancing in Treporti. The *vaporetto* only takes a quarter of an hour and then there is a bus. And once one is on the *terraferma* one has a choice of several places besides Treporti — there is Cà' Savio, and Cavallino, and even Jesolo if you want to go so far. Some of my friends are Communists and they organise a lot of activities. No, I am not a Communist, but I join in a lot of their activities.'

3 Torcello—A Fading Paradise

Torcello was one of the first of the islands in the lagoon to be permanently inhabited. Some traces of very early Roman structures have been discovered but they are probably the remains of salt-collectors' huts when they were working the nearby salt-pans in the marshes or of fishermen's shelters built for use in the spring and autumn fishing seasons. There are also traces of characteristic agriculture of the sixth and seventh century and some artisan activity, including the oldest indication yet found in the lagoon of a furnace for glass manufacturing.

Scholars do not seem quite to have made up their minds about the reasons for the flight of such large populations from the mainland. Barbarian hordes had, for generations before the earliest permanent settlement, been sweeping in from the north-east to the edge of the lagoon and devastating flourishing farm-lands and cities such as Altino. The permanent settlement dates from the sixth century only. It was in 639 that the bishop of Altino founded the great basilica of Santa Maria Assunta, having transferred the seat of the bishopric to Torcello. Given the discrepancy in dates, some historians have suggested that it was more a flight led by the bishop to protect those faithful to the Byzantine Christian rite from that propagated by the Lombards who were now settled in great strength all along the coast. If so, this was an ecclesiastical-political exodus and a prelude to the tremendous row, which broke out in 876 about the right to nominate the bishop of Torcello, which opposed the Church of Rome and the budding state of Venice. So the problem of the juridicial and political relations between Church and State which was to be such a troublesome element in Venetian history was raised at a very early stage.

The settlement in Torcello prospered. The prestige of a great church seems to have attracted settlers and by the year 1000 Torcello seems to have become perhaps the most important trading centre within the lagoon with a busy population of merchants, seamen and fishermen dealing in agricultural produce, fish and the beginnings of the wool trade. The main rival to Torcello was the settlement in Rialto and the neighbouring mesh of islands which was the nucleus of Venice. These islands gradually increased in population and influence at the expense of Torcello and other scattered island communities. There was more room in Venice and better access to the sea. The growth of the two settlements was accompanied by quarrels and conflicts dignified in legend by the name of wars. Later, when the supremacy of Venice was no longer in question, Torcello retained a certain measure of autonomy, with its own *podestà* and council, magistrature and system of nobility, all closely modelled on those of its powerful neighbour. Under the suzerainty of Venice Torcello administered the islands of Burano and Mazzorbo, and also Costanziaca and Ammiana which have long since disappeared beneath the waters of the lagoon as well as parts of the nearby *lidi*, presumably where Cavallino and Treporti now stand.

Until Napoleon ordered the dissolution of the monasteries in the Veneto, Torcello and the area it governed were chiefly in the ownership of the Church. Some of the monasteries and convents were independent foundations and some were what one might call country annexes of houses in Venice. In

141

Torcello itself there were at least seven foundations. There were many others in the smaller islands which have totally disappeared, such as Santa Cristina, and some which have left only the name of a canal, such as S. Felice or S. Lorenzo. The vanished island of Ammiana was said to have eight churches which implies a considerable ecclesiastical establishment. Of them all only S. Francesco del Deserto remains. Most of these convents had a chequered history, partly because piety varied along with the strictness of monastic discipline from age to age but also because tides and floods made buildings and land difficult to maintain, and because isolation and problems of transport discouraged even persistently devout communities.

That Torcello itself was always a summer paradise is clear from the number of villas which sprang up there. It was never an island of great country houses like those along the Brenta or scattered about the *terraferma*, but from the fifteenth century onwards there were summer residences surrounded by gardens and vineyards, cooled by the light breeze which comes from the sea as the sun goes down and by the flow of the tides. Gradually the canals silted up and with stagnant water came mosquitoes and malaria, and decay and depopulation.

John Ruskin writing in the middle of the nineteenth century describes the island thus:

Seven miles to the north of Venice, the banks of sand, which near the city rise little above low-water mark, attain by degrees a higher level, and knit themselves at last into fields of salt morass, raised here and there into shapeless mounds, and intercepted by narrow creeks of sea. One of the feeblest of these inlets, after winding for some time among buried fragments of masonry, and knots of sunburnt weeds whitened with webs of fucus, stays itself in an utterly stagnant pool beside a plot of greener grass covered with ground ivy and violets. On this mound is built a rude brick *campanile*, of the commonest Lombard type, which if we ascend towards evening (and there are none to hinder us, the door of its ruinous staircase swinging idly on its hinges), we may command from it one of the most notable

142

scenes in this wide world of ours. Far as the eye can reach, a waste of wild sea moor, of a lurid ashen grey; not like our northern moors with their jet-black pools and purple heath, but lifeless, the colour of sackcloth, with the corrupted sea-water soaking through the roots of its acrid weeds, and gleaming hither and thither through its snaky channels. No gathering of fantastic mists, nor coursing of clouds across it; but melancholy clearness of space in the warm sunset, oppressive, reaching to the horizon of its level gloom. To the very horizon, on the north-east; but to the north and west, there is a blue line of higher land along the border of it, and above this, but further back, a misty band of mountains, touched with snow. To the east, the paleness and roar of the Adriatic, louder at momentary intervals as the surf breaks on the bars of sand; to the south, the widening branches of the calm lagoon, alternately purple and pale green, as they reflect the evening clouds or twilight sky; and almost beneath our feet, on the same field which sustains the tower we gaze from, a group of four buildings, two of them a little larger than cottages (though built of stone, and one adorned with a quaint belfry), the third an octagonal chapel, of which we can see but little more than the flat red roof with its rayed tiling, the fourth, a considerable church with nave and aisles, but of which, in like manner, we can see little but the long central ridge and lateral slopes of roof, which the sunlight separates in one glowing mass from the green field beneath and the grey moor beyond. There are no living creatures near the buildings, nor any vestige of village or city around them. They lie like a little company of ships on a far-away sea.

This famous piece of mannered prose is almost as remarkable for what it leaves out as for what it puts in and is fascinating, too, as a glimpse of a purist recollecting emotions inaccurately in tranquillity. The most singular omission is that of human beings. Ruskin looking east to 'the paleness and roar of the Adriatic' (and what sharp ears he must have had, sharper than those of the modern inhabitants) could not but have seen the island of Burano crowded with little houses. A glance downwards would have shown him housing dating from the fifteenth to the eighteenth centuries belonging to Venetian patricians and the cottages where fishermen and *mezzadri* lived. Conditions were much the same at the end of the century as when Ruskin wrote, and then the parish was served by two priests. It was an extensive parish and besides Torcello itself with about 300 people included the islands of La Cura with 60 and Santa Cristina also with 60, as well as Lio Piccolo with something like 500. This does not sound like the unpopulated wastes, a kind of Arctic tundra, which Ruskin describes. It no doubt suited him to see the lagoon in the dark colours matching his liking for the medieval gloom of most gothic, though, in fact, Venetian gothic is of a relatively cheerful kind. His description sent me off to look again at Guardi who caught so admirably the play of light on the water in all its moods and at the lagoon itself which, nowadays, on a clear night with the navigation channels marked with orange lights, recalls the paintings by Whistler, and the flares of the Marghera oil refineries which have something of the subtle turbulence of Turner.

Since the decline of its mercantile prosperity and its absorption by Venice the islanders of Torcello have, on the whole, been *mezzadri*, that is, share-cropping peasants working for the landowners, though in the nineteenth century a few of them acquired small-holdings of their own. There has until quite recently been a sprinkling of fishermen among them but it is the peasants, the *contadini*, who have left their stamp on the community, at least since the dissolution of the monasteries. Compared with the population of Burano, the *contadini* were well off. In terms of money they were as poor, but not as disastrously poor because they were better fed. 'The land is very precious,' as one of them said. There are still one or two families who feed themselves from the produce of their little fields and gardens, especially if the older members of the family have been *contadini*. They are careful people and if the land can produce the fruit, vegetables, eggs and poultry to feed them they do not buy it in the shops. In spite of this the housewives of Torcello make almost daily shopping trips to Burano, largely to satisfy the

144

expectations of the younger members for a more varied diet, and particularly for more meat. As one of these matrons told me: 'They expect every day the sort of meals we had at weddings.'

The soil in the lagoon islands is fertile. A report issued on agriculture in Italy for the international congress on agriculture held in 1878 said that 'along the coast [of the Veneto] and particularly in the Venetian lagoon the arable soil has no great depth but a very high fertility and is extremely rich in humus; but, in a number of places, the peasants are obliged to build banks to preserve their fields from the invasion of water at the time of the high tides of the autumn and winter.'

Torcello, Mazzorbo, the Vignole and the neighbouring *terraferma* are the traditional suppliers of the market of Rialto. 'Nostrano' (our own produce) is the cry one constantly hears even today when a growing resident and tourist population make it of doubtful truth. The lagoon islands are favoured by their position. They are sheltered by the *lidi* from the main force of gales yet, being surrounded by sea, they get little frost and, more important for the vine and tomato harvest, few hailstorms. The difference between the sea and the land temperature leads to the precipitation of violent and destructive local hailstorms all along the Cavallino peninsula. In a normal year the *contadini* of the islands can expect to have their crops ready for market two weeks or so before the *terraferma* and cash in on the higher prices prevailing at the beginning of a season.

The crops for which Torcello has long been famous are peaches and artichokes. Before the great flood of April 1936, which reached the height of 1.51 metres, the second highest ever recorded in the long tally kept by the Serene Republic, the island was a blaze of peach-blossom in the spring and the fruit much prized. They were medium only in size but of a delicious taste and fragrance. They stood up admirably to travel and so could be picked almost ripe and sent to far markets, some of them outside Italy. The great majority of these peach trees were killed by the high flood waters of 1936. The *contadini* say that since then fruit-trees, indeed trees of any size, do not last for many years. It is difficult to understand why. It may perhaps be that the water table has risen and that the long deep roots of large trees penetrate into salt-laden layers of soil. Certainly if you dig a hole a metre deep in Torcello it will fill up with water in a few hours. On the other hand, at San Francesco del Deserto there are many large trees, mostly cypresses but also deciduous trees such as limes whose roots must also go into the salt layers, though it is true that the land there lies higher than in Torcello. Artichoke plants fear frost and sea-water but have a long life if protected from these hazards. The best protection against frost is to bend the plant towards the south and make a hump of earth on the other side to shield it from the bitter north wind, or *bora* as they call it in Venice. There is no protection against sea-water if it breaks through the banks and the great flood of November 1966 which drowned the fields to a depth of three or four feet killed every artichoke plant in the island. This was a major calamity since artichoke plants do not begin to bear until they are two years old.

In normal times artichokes are a good paying crop. Those of Torcello are particularly sought after for their delicacy and flavour, and the early *castruga*, which is the top bud of the plant with long tender leaves, can bring in 60 or 70 lire to the grower and sells in the shops for anything up to 200 lire. Then in descending order of delicacy and price and produced as the season lengthens come the *primo bottolo*, the *carcioffo*, the *articioco* and finally the *fondo*, the artichoke heart which you see all ready prepared floating about in tubs in Italian greengrocers' shops. The cultivation of artichokes requires skill, constant attention and hard work. The mounds built in the autumn to protect the heart of the plant from frost have to be demolished in the spring, the excess shoots or *figli* (children) have to be pulled out, and the plant tidied and manured and tended from time to time throughout the growing season. The artichokes have to be picked, sorted, packed, despatched and sometimes also transported to the mainland for delivery to more distant markets. When the year's growth has died down at the end of the summer the old stalks have to be pulled out to make room for the new growth which will have to be protected from frost. It is a great deal of work for very little reward. An expert grower

146

with a competent knowledge of marketing may average out at 20 or 15 lire an artichoke. Some only get 7 or 8 lire. On a small holding of five acres it is not possible to keep a family at such prices. One land-owner summed up the problem thus:

> When I first came to Torcello there were 250 inhabitants and the land was all under cultivation. Bit by bit the young men went away. The land no longer produced so much, particularly after the 1936 floods, but the *contadini* chiefly left because they got too little for their produce at market. They could not live. This is a disaster because the land is excellent. Torcello is very fertile. There are now only two or three well-kept holdings left and they produce first-class produce. The problem is to ensure selling at a price which will keep a family.

The conditions of the *contadini* in the lagoon islands are those facing the whole of Italy, made perhaps more difficult by the cost and slowness of water transport, which restricts the number of markets to which produce can be sent. Among these conditions the *mezzadria* or share-cropping system was one of the worst. Now, no new contracts can be made but old contracts have still to be worked out. Long ago there were advantages in the system. It provided security for the *contadini* and a reasonable return on his capital for the land-owner, and at a time when prices were stable and expectations low probably worked well enough. But in the long run it proved a cruel and destructive system fraught with resentments and accusations of bad faith and at its worst a reflection of the selfishness of property-owners, which leads to revolution. And even if the land-owner kept strictly and generously to his part of the contract, it was not he, but the *contadini*, who went hungry in a bad year. I know of only one *mezzadro* in the lagoon who says of his land-owner, '*E buono, buono, mio padrone.*' Relations between the few remaining others range from dislike and fear to something near hatred and contempt.

The *mezzadria* system had two unforeseen consequences. One is that, as the owner had never paid his *mezzadro* a wage, he came to think that the work was not worth paying for. This kept agricultural salaries low, with all the consequent feelings of inferiority and lack of status as compared with other workers. The *contadini*, paid the normal wages, can scarcely live unless he has some land of his own. He then has to cultivate two lots of land and grow and market two lots of crops. This is killing work and it is small wonder that he looks for other employment. The second consequence is the abandonment of the land, as the cost of the social security contributions combined with the low prices of produce make agriculture, except on a large scale, a doubtful economic proposition. So the owner tends to let the land go to ruin. Fifteen years ago in Torcello there were flourishing vineyards, orchards, plantations of artichokes, tomatoes, aubergines, zucchini, lettuces, peas and beans. There are now tangles of grass, mosquito-infested ditches of stagnant water and thickets of reeds marching further every year into the rare cultivated fields. Ruskin's description may come to be true a hundred years after he wrote it. A Torcellano said:

Nobody wants to work the land any more. They all want a regular monthly wage and agriculture is too chancy. There were two gardens here which were well worked. One belonged to Cipriani's *locanda*. It is about five acres and supplies the restaurant besides sending produce to Venice. Beautifully kept. The other belonged to that Englishwoman at the Cà' S. Tomà. It produced good stuff. Both these gardens were run by men on monthly salaries and both of them had land of their own so they were all right and could make ends meet. All *contadini* should have a monthly wage. It is the only way. You cannot expect a man to go on growing spinach to sell at 10 lire a kilo when you pay 200 lire a kilo in the shops. Yes, working the land is a satisfaction but, *poverini*, they must be able to live.

A land-owner said:

Small private land-owners cannot pay the salaries and the huge social security contributions. No, no, no, they cannot do it. At present prices the harvest does not cover costs let alone bring in any profit. And anyway the young men do not want to work on the land and you cannot run a vineyard on the old men who are left. They have the skill, certainly, but they no longer have the strength to work all day under a broiling sun. It is not only Torcello that is decaying. It is same in the Vignole which is gradually being abandoned. Good marketing and protection for the small-holdings are the only solution. On the *terraferma* the problem is different. There you can, if you can get round the inheritance laws which divide up the land into small parcels, throw holdings together and make an economically viable holding. But these islands have no room. And then, they hang on to their land even if it is only big enough to grow a lettuce, even if they don't want to grow a lettuce.

So there is an enduring love of the land in spite of discouragement among those who work it. There is an almost desperate pursuit of new ideas, of some magical formula which will somehow increase the yield of crops. One man will try out a new method and if it is successful it will be copied by everyone in the district with little understanding of the technology involved, of its advantages and disadvantages, of the use and abuse of fertilisers and insecticides. A case in point is the use of nylon structures to bring on crops faster and protect them from bad weather. The countryside round Treporti is now covered with nylon *serre* without much knowledge of the management of these expensive structures. The *contadini* thereabouts are like sorcerers' apprentices boiling up a spell, and their expenditure in money, work and heartbreak when diseases ruin their crop and hailstorms rip up their nylon covers swing them back to disillusion and despair. How can they launch their children, provide a better house, care for their wives and mothers when the spell never turns out right?

The *contadini* of the lagoon need a good agricultural advisory service. They exist in Italy. The nearest one is perhaps the State Agricultural Institute in Castelfranco on the *terraferma* which, however, belongs to a different administrative region. It is fashionable to say that the *contadino* (indeed the Italian, in general) will not co-operate even for his own obvious good. But the Castelfranco institute has proved the contrary. Under skilful leadership the *contadini* there are beginning to venture out of the extended family circle, that fortress which buttresses you in evil days and rejoices with you in the good and at all times shelters you from the sharp winds of the world outside. Gradually — and it is a long process — the advantages of at least minimal co-operation begin to be appreciated by small-holders, who cannot by themselves finance large expenditure or organise profitable marketing. The island people are no different and their circumstances, if anything, more difficult because of the lagoon.

The price a *contadino* gets for his produce is the key to the survival of small agriculture and in the lagoon it is, necessarily, all small agriculture. One constantly hears it said in Torcello and the other islands that the soil is so fertile that a good worker could make a very reasonable living out of quite a small holding if he could be sure of a reasonable price. The disparity between the price paid to the *contadino* and the price the public pays in the shops is the main cause of resentment and discontent. This could at least be mitigated by ensuring through market controls that the grower received a larger proportion of the price. If a *contadino* is only paid 5 to 8 lire for an artichoke the total he receives for a small boatload does not, at present prices, pay for the petrol he uses to take them to market in Venice, let alone for his time and labour. As one of them said:

In Mussolini's day the peasant got a fair price for his produce. He made a law by which the peasant got half the market price. We would not want him back, he did some dreadful things, but I must say, he did give the peasants a chance to make a living.

This is an argument which would bear watching by those with a care for democracy because, in the present confused times, it would be easy to exploit it for political ends.

Torcello today has seventy-five inhabitants and is not capable of keeping any one of them entirely on the island's own resources. One or more members of each family has a job elsewhere, usually in Burano, Murano or on the *terra-ferma*, which brings in a regular wage. It is a curious thought that the many thousands of tourists who come every year to visit the great basilica of Santa Maria Assunta, the charming Byzantine church of Santa Fosca and the village *piazza,* have no impact at all on the society which they so rapidly traverse. By the early evening they have all gone. The stall-holders who sell glass and lace and postcards have also gone, for not even they are local people. The island belongs again to the Torcellani, their dogs and cats and ducks and the guests dining in the garden of Cipriani's. And if they go for a walk afterwards on the further banks edging the *palude* they might have the luck to see a heron fishing or even a nightingale trying out his song. But both are retreating into the far-off *valli.* In a sense, the famous monuments belong more to the tourists than to the local population who seldom set foot in them. Mass is attended by a very sparse sprinkling of Torcellani, and the school, that other potent agent of social cohesion, has ceased to exist. Its life as a school was short. For many years children were taught in a borrowed room and often in the church itself, which must have pleased the passing ghost of any medieval wandering scholar. Then President Einaudi became interested in Torcello and arranged for proper school buildings in a house next door to Cipriani's *locanda.* By that time the population was already dwindling and the younger people, particularly the parents of primary school age children, were moving away to other jobs, and the number of pupils was reduced to two when the time came for the school-mistress to retire. She was not replaced and the children (who now number eight or ten because of a new large family who came to Torcello and marriages amongst the tiny population) go to school in Burano with free passes on the *vaporetto.*

The bridge (in a sense the buffer) between the people of Torcello and the outside world is Cipriani's *locanda* and it would be difficult to exaggerate its importance in the life of the island. It required imagination and vision backed by technical expertise of a high order to perceive in the rather dreary little country inn squatting at the turn of the canal the possibilities of creating a restaurant which has acquired world renown for standards in food, in rustic elegance, in courtesy of welcome, in skilful, unobtrusive service, and for its garden full of flowers and lettuces leading the eye over the

151

roof of Santa Fosca to the bulk of the basilica and the sturdy campanile. The man who possessed these qualities of vision and judgment was Commendatore Giuseppe Cipriani. For some, the importance of Torcello depends on the splendour of its monuments. For many more it is Cipriani's. Without the *locanda* Torcello could be rather squalid. Too many visitors, too many tourist stalls, too much take and too little give, as is nowadays unfortunately normal in the world of tourism. Its presence rights the balance.This tidy, modest, characteristic exterior gives substance, a feeling of the genuine and the real to the approaches of the *piazza* which could so easily escape into the meretricious and the tawdry. This is a purely visual matter and has nothing to do with whether one can afford to eat there or not. But the import- ance of Cipriani's to Torcello extends much further. It springs from a love and a sense of responsibility for the island and its people. The day-to-day running of the *locanda* has, from the start, been in the hands of the Signorina Gabriella, who is the sister-in-law of the founder, and it was she who chiefly gave effect to this sense of responsibility, whether it was bringing together people who could help the island and conserve the monuments, aiding a concert in the basilica, suggesting the restoration of Galuppi to the church music of his native islands, or doing so many kindnesses to strangers and locals alike, including providing summer employment which made all the difference to a local boy's being able to finish his university course, and giving a polish to his waiter's training which took another local boy to a job in a great hotel in London and the management of a restaurant there. The point of cohesion in the community of Torcello is undoubtedly the Signorina Gabriella. The Cipriani family have given to the island more than it can ever know.

They bought the old inn and had it put into sufficient order to receive a few clients before the war broke out, when it had to be closed. In 1943 it was possible to begin the slow process of assembling the materials for repairs (the wood for the beams and other internal work was brought down from Cadore up in the mountains) and for modernising the structure.

The *locanda* was opened on May 5, 1946, with an invitation lunch. As always the builders had not finished and had to be turned out. The entire staff consisted of a cook and a *sommelier* and the Signorina Gabriella, and between them they did everything. At first there was only one room and that the Signorina occupied during the months the *locanda* was open. It seems to have prospered from the first, justifying the imagination that saw the opportunity. But what courage and what hard work must have been required to solve all the normal problems which confront a new restaurant so far from sources of supplies and extra staff, and at the same time to ensure high standards and to watch costs.

In November 1948 Ernest Hemingway and his wife Mary spent a month at Cipriani's while he was writing *Over the River and into the Trees*. They are remembered with warm affection. He, robust, difficult, hard-drinking and hard-working; she, greatly loved, interested in local folk-songs, helpful to him in his writing. He loved and understood the lagoon and used to go out duck shooting with the gardener, Emilio. As the *locanda's* reputation grew, many famous people travelled there. President Einaudi of Italy came; so, too, during the conference of the Christian Democratic party held in Venice, did many of the leaders and members of the government. At that time Cipriani's was the only house with electricity and the party conference was met with signs painted up along the canal, '*Vogliamo la luce*' (we want light), and it was installed within a week. At this point the schoolchildren took a hand and wrote saying that there ought to be a proper shelter from the rain and wind at the *vaporetto* landing stage. This took a little longer but within a month work had started on building a rather pleasant rural structure which (with some renovations) is still in use today. Later Queen Elizabeth and the Duke of Edinburgh came when the *Britannia*, anchored in the Bacino between St. Mark's and San Giorgio Maggiore, was causing considerable excitement in Venice. Still later, Nancy Mitford spent several weeks there finishing a book.

To prosper, or even to continue to exist, a community must surely have, or be able to create, a tradition, have a means to earn its keep and be of a sufficient size to provide a feeling of belonging. If this is so, it is difficult to see a future for Torcello. It has a long tradition but, in recent centuries at least, it has been a dependent society, dependent for its living on patricians, ecclesiastical or lay land-owners whom it served. It has acquired, perhaps because of this past, a softer, gentler outlook than its robust neighbour, Burano. It lacks that inch of steel that comes from adversity. It is not that Torcello has not seen difficult times. In agriculture there seem always to be more hard times than good and the island, almost surrounded by *palude* (flats just covered at high tide), has suffered very severely from malaria. The people have been poor but they have not starved. Agriculture was its only possible economic basis. Intensive market gardening with the most up-to-date techniques, including sophisticated marketing and a national system of transporting produce (instead of small *topetti* and *sandali* taking individual crops long distances), could still save this society. The skills are there and the men could even now be attracted back to the land, but there is no incentive for land-owners to find the capital for as long as low prices pertain for agricultural produce.

So the people continue to drift away. The population has for some time now been too small to provide the clash of variety and contrast which gives vision and vitality to a community. The interests of the inhabitants now lie outside Torcello: their jobs, their amusements and, increasingly, their families and friends. Torcello, for the native Torcellani, is becoming a dormitory and not a very convenient dormitory at that, with a church which means little in their lives and not even a school to help keep them together. It is a dying community.

Various suggestions have been made to save it. One was to parcel up the land into little lots where cottages could be built for workers with jobs in the lagoon. But this kind of half-way house would not rebuild a community. The idea was shouted down by those who love the solitude of the island (while taking good care not to live in it) and did not greatly appeal to those for whom it was designed. So, like many ideas in Venice, it created much talk before being quietly buried.

The most probable future for Torcello is that the few houses still occupied by Torcellani will gradually be bought up by rich foreigners or Italians for use as summer residences. A number are already empty for most of the year and the land is kept tidy but unproductive. From the point of view of the summer visitor this is more agreeable than fields overrun with reeds and silted-up canals harbouring mosquitoes. Because of rising costs and wages, it will never become the well-manicured, shampooed countryside that delights the rich man's eye. It will be the end of Torcello as a community. It is dying and, within the lifetime of people now becoming old, it will be dead. It will become a site with marvellous monuments — a sort of out-door museum. At least one will be able to get a good lunch.

Three People on the Land

She is one of the dignified matrons of this gentle island. She takes an evident pride in coming from a long line of Torcellani. She has all the solid characteristics of a country woman. She can milk a cow and hoe a row of artichokes, and prune a tree and harvest the grapes and kill a hen and cook and bake and sew and patch and has done and has had to do all these things in her time. She has a satirical vein which flashes out in comic and merciless comments on people and affairs, combined with a twinkle and a sense of fun, a gentleness and courtesy and affection towards her friends and a tower of strength in times of trouble. She has brought up four children of her own and has stood by and made sacrifices for a number of less fortunate children and relatives. Her temper has not been spoilt by adversity though perhaps that thread of steel in her character which shows itself in a severity about standards is more in evidence than it would have been had life been easier. She is one of the more remarkable of that race, *la mamma*, which is one of the strengths of these islands. An unexpected side of her is seen when she is in her *sandalo*. One suddenly sees the young woman who won so many races in regattas. With a slight shift of weight and a turn of the wrist she drives forward and manoeuvres her boat apparently without effort. It is beautiful to watch.

'When we were children we had very little time to play, very little. Either we were at school, or doing jobs around the house or in the fields. One of the jobs given to the little children was scaring sparrows away from the fruit and particularly the vines when they were ripening in the autumn. I have spent weeks with the other children down in the vineyards shouting and singing and running about and making a clatter with strips of laths tied loosely together to scare off the birds. However, we enjoyed it. It wasn't real work.

We used also to have fun going swimming. All of us children went together and we were encouraged to go by our parents because we really had to know how to swim. It was we children who had to go with the boat and fetch the water and we really had to know how to swim because we were always falling in. I don't ever remember not being able to swim and not being able to row.

Both in Torcello and Burano fetching the water was a job for the children. I was six or seven when they started sending me and another child to fetch the water. We kept cows so we needed a lot of water. We had a boat where the two water butts were kept and when the water got low we two had to go and fill them up. We would row down to the fountain (it is still there outside Cipriani's *locanda*) and fix a little rubber tube on to the oulet pipe of the fountain and fill the butts. We must have lost dozens of these rubber tubes in the canal and, of course, we had to go in after them to try to get them back and, of course, that improved our swimming. The work was a bit heavy when we were so young but we were strong and once we got the boat moving along it was not too difficult. But it all took time. Once we had to row over to Mazzorbo and coming back with the water butts full we ran into a choppy sea out there in the lagoon and we shipped a lot of water and the boat sank. We had to swim to the *barena* and from there we had to wade back soaking wet and with mud to our middles. *Mamma mia*, did we get into trouble! When the wind dropped my father and another man had to go out and salvage the boat, and in the meantime we did not have any water at home and, worse still, the animals didn't have any either.

At this time we used to be sent to bed while the sun was still up. It wasn't so much that we had to get up early but that there were so many of us children about that the grown-ups wanted a bit of peace. The men and women wanted to be alone without all of us around. So we were given our supper early and *via* off we were sent to bed. When the men came in from work the children were already in bed. Even if we were working in the fields or round the house we were called in and packed off to bed before the men got back. Mind you, sometimes I used to creep downstairs and listen to the grown-ups talking. I was the only one to do it, the others were too scared. You ask my cousin about it, she'll remember.

But we did play. We had a game called "the devil". Some people called it the "black man". When the "he" shouted "Who's afraid of the devil — or of the black man", we all cried "Nobody" and ran as fast as we could round the pond we had near the house and the devil or black man would try to catch us. And there again, we were always falling in. We had another game called *al pangalo* which we played with little sticks. We hit the little sticks with a sort of a bat to see who could hit furthest. We had another game which was very popular and which we called *I morti* (the dead men). *I morti* were little pebbles and the game was to shift them along the ground by bouncing other pebbles at them. We had to invent our games. We didn't have toys or dolls. We didn't have anything. The children nowadays still play our old games though, of course, they have toys and all sorts of things we never had. We did have a bit of rope, though, and used to play skipping and singing games which children now still use.

But even if we did not have much time to play we joined in all the feasts and great occasions. Everybody in Torcello kept pigs and it was a great day when we killed them. We all killed on the same day and held a great party. We killed towards the end of November, or maybe it was the first Sunday in December. It must have been about November 27. We listened very carefully when the priest read the lesson and when we heard him say, "There is come amongst you one whom you do not know", we knew the time had come to kill the pig. Now, when the pig is killed, it is still an occasion but less so than before. People kill their pig when it is convenient now, not all on the same day as before. It was so much gayer when we all did it together. It was *una vera festa* (a real party).

As the girls got older they had to help more in the house, with the cooking and cleaning and laundry. I remember we used to use the ash of artichoke plants to whiten the linen. We used to put a handful of artichoke ash into the boiler. You had to be careful not to put too much in because it could be strong and could burn your hands and make holes in the sheets. But if you put in just enough the sheets came out white, white and sweet-smelling, better than with today's washing powders. Of course, it was more work.

One of the first things I learned to cook was artichokes in the traditional Torcellana fashion. For this you must have small, young artichokes. You take off the outside leaves, cut off the spiky ends and slice off the stalk end so that each artichoke stands up by itself. When properly prepared each one

158

is about an inch high. Now you stand them all up so that they fill the bottom of a saucepan, salt and pepper them, pour in a good quantity of olive oil and enough water to cover them. Put them on a low fire and let them cook slowly. You can eat them either hot or cold. You really need Torcello artichokes which are famous for their delicate taste. We used to make a winter provision of artichokes, too, *carciofi sott'olio*. We prepared the artichokes in the same way as for cooking but they must be even smaller and more tender, and then you bottle them and they are very useful when there are no vegetables in the garden.

Here in Torcello we eat better than they do in Burano. They have got fish over there but so have we. In addition, we have gardens and we like to have everything fresh and picked ripe. We do not like fruit picked before it is ripe in order to be sent to market. We do not think it has any taste. We like to pick our fruit and vegetables right out of the garden on to the table or into the pot.

In the autumn we get wild duck (mallard) and, of course, there are people in Burano that shoot, too. It is getting difficult to find duck these days. They say that it is because there are fewer marshes for the birds, but whatever the reason they are becoming rare which is a pity because they are so good. Most people do not know how to cook them. Duck live on fish and so they taste fishy if they are not properly cooked. Most people try to cover up the taste of fish by marinading the duck in vinegar and water or making a strong sauce. The right way to do it is to prick the skin in many places, being careful not to stick the needle beyond the fat that lies under the skin into the flesh. Then you put the bird into a moderate oven until all the fat just beneath the skin has run out into the pan. It is this fat that tastes fishy and this is the way to get rid of it. After that you can roast the bird whole or cut it into pieces and braise it. We eat *polenta* with duck because there is always excellent juice from the bird.

But all this time the most important thing for me was school. I did five years' schooling up to the fifth class and then I did one more year after my certificate. Six years' schooling from the age of six years. In Burano few people of my generation know how to read or write — very few — particularly the women. In Torcello the people value education more and were always after the children to make them work properly at school. My mother was certainly always after me, and my brothers all went on to the sixth and seventh class. In those days schools were not divided up into junior and senior secondary as it is now, but what my brothers had was a secondary education. I did the sixth year but I had to leave in the middle of the seventh to start work. Now the children have to do eight years but I think it is still not enough, but then I am a real Torcellana where education is concerned. One of the reasons why the children of Torcello could continue with school when the Buranelli could not was because of the difference in the sort of work children were expected to do at home. Our work in Torcello was in the house or at the door or in the vineyard, and we could get it done early in the morning and then go off to school. That was not possible in Burano. There the boys were needed for the fishing and you have to fish according to the tides and the weather, and often at night, so it was not possible to keep school hours as well. With us the work was on our doorstep. It was daytime work and what you could not do now you can usually do later. Quite different. It enabled our boys to get more schooling.

Fishing was important to us. Every year *bragoze* came sailing up from Chioggia to fish in the *barene* hereabouts. My uncle, my mother's brother-in-law, used to come up every September to fish *cefali* (grey mullet) *anghuea* (whitebait) and *moleche* (little shore crabs), fished and sold immediately after moulting in the spring and autumn. My uncle, like many others, used to row up from Chioggia in small boats. It used to take hours, nobody would think of doing it these days. Each boat had a crew of three, a man and two boys. Six or seven boats, mostly belonging to brothers or relatives, would fish together and take it in turns to take all the catch to the Rialto market in Venice while the others got on with the fishing. They would stay up at this end of the lagoon for five or six weeks or even for two months, living all the time in their rowing boats. My aunt used to make the bread they called *busoei*. My aunt had an oven and made

160

sacks of it before they left. It was mostly stored in the boats in pillowcases. *Busoei* lasts very well. It lasts for months because it has the consistency of biscuit and is so good, so good. They still make it in Chioggia. There are still a few boats which come up for this fishing but not many are left. They are mostly the sons or nephews who have taken over. This sort of fishing is called *mistieretti* because it was a small boat trade and they never went out of the lagoon into the open sea, unlike the *bragoze,* which are large sea-going fishing smacks. The crews of the *bragoze* were also mostly brothers or relatives. The *bragoze* used to come up in fleets of ten or so at a time and we used to buy the cast-off shells of the *moleche* to use as fertiliser on the artichokes. They make excellent fertiliser.

When I left school I helped my father on our holding. We grew vegetables of all kinds, particularly the famous Torcello artichokes, and one of my jobs was to take them to market at the Rialto in Venice. Depending on the weather and the tide, it took three to four hours to row from Torcello to the Grand Canal. Often I had to leave at two o'clock in the morning and, of course, I was alone. There was no room for anyone else in a heavy-laden *sandalo. Mamma mia,* how frightened I used to be, particularly when I had to row in the dark along by the cemetery with its dark cypresses and the wind moaning along the wall. With two oars to manage I did not even have a free hand to cross myself. *Mamma mia!* I have always been a good strong rower, in fact, I used to win rowing races at the regattas and am still very fond of rowing and often take the *sandalo* over to Burano. I used to row as fast as I could past the cemetry. Then during the war, when the fort at the entrance to the Mazzorbo canal, opposite the old cemetery, was occupied by soldiers, I used to be so frightened in case they shot me. *"Qui vive?"* they used to challenge and I used to answer in a small voice, *"Sono io"* (it's me), and finally they got used to me and laughed when I answered. But I was frightened just the same.

We lived very well. In fact, before the war we thought we were very well off compared with the people of Burano, who were so very poor at that time. But with our land and so many children old enough to do really useful work in the fields and the vineyards, and with the good prices we got for our produce, we lived well in a modest way. Now a family could hardly live on such a small holding because prices for agricultural products are so low and so much goes to the middle man. Mostly peasants worked the land as *mezzadri* in those days but even so they were able to make a living for themselves as well as a good return for the owner of the land. After the war the *mezzadria* system was abolished but there are still a few old arrangements going on.

If you had land you always ate properly, poultry, pigs, rabbits, ducks, fruit and vegetables. We were not rich, not at all rich, but we seemed to be happy. When I was young we used to have very happy outings in the boats, young people all together. We used to go for miles in the lagoon — right over to Cason Bianco sometimes and to Capo Sile.

Just after the war there was a hard period. When I was a young married woman with three little children we took in my brother's five children. We couldn't let them go to an orphanage. That made ten of us altogether and things were not easy. One winter we had only *polenta* and dried figs to eat. You can imagine what that diet did to the children's insides. I had one or other of them ill all the time and sometimes more than one, and there was I trying to nurse them and help in the fields as usual because I was needed there too. *Maria Vergine*, what a hard time that was. It has left its mark on us too.

Life began to get easier in the sixties, well after the war, when the industries started in Murano and Mestre. People began to work outside Burano and Torcello. That was quite new and it made a big difference, to the people of Burano especially. In Torcello life stayed about the same. Before then, life in Burano was *magra* (thin) but in Torcello, as I said, things were not too bad because we had the land. It is very precious, you know. They don't even have little gardens in Burano, only a few pots with flowers in the courtyard. It is just like Venice, they don't have the space.

Things have changed a lot with more jobs and better wages. Of course, people expect more than we used to but even with crises (and now we've got another one!) things are better for most people. The things that have changed most are clothing, food, amusements. When we were very little we were always afraid. There was nobody to answer for us or take charge of us. We were afraid of the *vigili* and *carabinieri* (police of different kinds), of everything, and now it is quite another life. Then it was an occasion to go to mass. When I was a child we put on shoes on Sundays to go to church. On other days we went barefoot or in winter we wore *papousette*. My sister used to make them with pieces of stuff sewn on to a leather sole. We also used to make our own clogs, *galosi* we used to call them, or *gazocoli*. My father shaped a bit of wood for the sole and on top we would nail a piece of leather or sometimes of sailcloth and *via!* All these were made at home and we thought them luxurious!

Machines, too, have made our lives much easier out here in the lagoon, particularly outboard motors for the fishermen and light tractors for the peasants. But we have only had these things since the sixties. Before that life was very hard.

We are very different from the people of Burano even if we are only five or six minutes away in a rowing boat. For instance, in Burano they say they are related to I don't know how many degrees of kinship. Those people set great store by the family. It means a lot to them and they hang on to them even when they are right outside all the recognised degrees. It must be because they have all been there since the world began. They have got used to one another. We, here in Torcello, certainly we love our families, our parents and children, cousins and aunts and so on, but family relationships matter less to us outside these degrees. But the Buranello really clings to them all. Everybody is related to everybody else over there and they like it that way.'

If, towards the end of summer, you catch a late-night *vaporetto*, you will see, as you approach the *pontile*, a stocky female figure standing below the light and peering into the water. She is usually quite still, with her weight on one leg, leaning on a long pole topped with a wide wire net. Beside her on the deck is a bucket squirming with the night's catch of *calamaretti*, little squids angrily squirting ink over one another. Suddenly she takes a quick step forward and

163

with a flick of the wrist plunges the net into the water, scoops up a school of *calamaretti*, decants it into the bucket and returns to her position of vigilant inactivity until the next school drifts by in the cloudy water. Her movements are so fast and so brief that it is only the drips of water on the pontoon deck that convince you that she has actually moved. If you ask her what her catch is worth she will say: 'That lot? Umm, perhaps ten thousand lire. It will pay for my evening's pleasure, ho, ho!'

She is perhaps fifty and her passions are music and fishing and the progress of her more musical nephews and nieces. She is good with her hands and is to be found mending shoes, household articles, electric irons, always to the sound of music. She only breaks off work to change a record or switch to another radio station. She chiefly likes opera and lives swaddled in arias from *Aida* or *Tosca*. She is outspoken and indestructably cheerful and has a rough, no-nonsense manner which hides an absurdly tender heart. She uses the old-fashioned greeting: *'Salve.'* This is what she told me:

'We have always been peasants, though my father sometimes went road-mending to make ends meet. We were nine children in the family and we all lived in one room and a kitchen. Fine conditions to raise children in. We did not have any money but at least we were all healthy and the times were better than they are now with all the harassments and violence of today. Look at the way people behave these days. They didn't when we were young. We had two or three fields and we managed to live. The little children went to the kindergarten and the bigger ones to school and our mother went to work for our uncles who had a bit more land than we did. Every day she brought back something to help out at home, some flour, a bit of fruit, some wood. If you only have a little land, you cannot expect to have enough wood for your needs, and all our cooking and heating was done by wood. A barbarous life it was, a dog's life, that's what.

We got such schooling as we could. Three of us (two girls and a boy) got as far as the fifth class and the rest managed to get to the third or the second class. I did three years of school and that was the lot, but then I went to night school and completed the fifth class and got my certificate.

I began working when I was twelve. I went into domestic service. All three of us sisters became domestics at the age of twelve, two of us in Venice and one on the *terraferma*. We had to live with the families where we were employed, and sometimes we got home on our free days and sometimes we could bring something to help out at home — a little flour, some dried beans, that sort of thing. But the war was on, you know, and there was not much to spare. My wages were 500 lire a month but, of course, I was fed. I did not stay long in that job but became an assistant in a grocer's shop near home. I was there for a long time.

It must have been in the early fifties that we moved house and came to live here. Then everybody came back from their various jobs to help because if a hoe is your only tool to till the fields you need a good many people with hoes. My mother also lived with us and prepared our food. At lunch time one of us would go back to the house to fetch it in a basket and we would eat it in the fields where we were working. Our drink was water with a little vinegar in it. We never had wine. We never saw bread. Our main food was *polenta*, you know, made of maize.

This land we cultivated, this land we are standing on, was a new *bonifica*, that is, land won back from the lagoon. All

165

this had been *palude*. The only solid bit was this thin bank retaining the canal and which we call an *intraio*. You have to let a newly reclaimed land lie fallow for a while to get rid of the salt because the lagoon, as you know, is sea-water. Then you can start planting. All this land along the canal and right across to the lagoon is *bonifica* and there was nothing growing here, except some sedge, when we came. All these vines and all these trees were planted by us. The first crop we planted was *panocie* (maize). We put the whole lot under maize for several years to have *polenta* for ourselves and also to sell. We were one of several families working here and, of course, none of us owned the land we worked. The proprietor divided it up into lots and made a contract with each family. All the families went to work planting potatoes and maize. Then we put in vines and peach trees. Now that everything is bearing it brings in quite a good return for our work, that is to say it would if it were not a *mezzadria*. And it is still held by us as a *mezzadria*. We get fifty-eight per cent of the crop and the owner gets forty-two per cent, and the toil and burden is all ours. The owner did provide part of a tractor to be hired by all of us when required, but the terms were so difficult that we got fed up and bought our own, hire-purchase, of course, we couldn't have managed otherwise. But at least we could get on with our work. We live, we live better than when I was a child, but you can't say we live well. This land eats us all up. This was new land here, not belonging to anyone. It was all acquired by one of these "barons" who know how to fiddle things and here we are all stuck with *mezzadria* contracts. They are absolutely forbidden but the old contracts made before the law was passed are still valid. They should all have been swept away. The Parliament should have done a better job. The peasant should be able to live at about the same standard as a skilled worker in other trades. You see all of them with their cars. If we are lucky we have a bicycle, otherwise we go on our feet. It is still a struggle to live. We are much better off than we were before, at least we are not eleven in a room. Here we have rooms to ourselves. Of course, the whole family doesn't work and live here any more. Some brothers have gone off to other jobs and sisters to get married.

The young ones in the family won't stay on the land. Now compulsory schooling lasts eight years and after all that study they feel able to do better for themselves than working on the land and off they go. And I see why. It is hard work and apart from that one doesn't have the will to work the land any more. There is no satisfaction in it. My nephews and nieces are still young and we do not yet know what they will want to do in life except, of course, my niece who is studying the flute and a nephew who has already completed his course. The French horn is his instrument and he is already a member of an orchestra which has given concerts in Paris and Innsbruck and other places abroad. He loves the lagoon, and particularly fishing, and comes out here whenever he can.'

*

Giulindo is a man of forty-three married to a local girl and with three children. All his life he has worked on the land and, by skill and thrift and the help of a wife who shares his combination of toughness, kindness and flexibility, has the satisfaction at least of owning his own piece of land and building a good, modern house. He can now expect to launch his son into whatever way of life he chooses. Without the help of a formal education (he had only three years' primary schooling before beginning to share the burden of gaining daily bread for a family of fatherless children) he has a capacity to think and reflect and to act on his reflection. Sometimes the seeming miracles of scientific agriculture have led him astray and disappointed hopes pitched too high, but a solidity of character and a resignation burnt into him by a difficult childhood have pulled him through the depression caused by the loss of time and work and hard-earned money. He has a sturdy independence, a self-confidence amounting sometimes to a distrust (acquired in a hard school) of any but his own family and closest friends, an exactness of conscience and an integrity of behaviour allied to a capacity for hard work which make him a good farmer, a good associate and a good friend.

167

'My grandfather had one of the *valli* (enclosures for raising fish for market) in the Sacchetti which lies just beyond the island of Saccagnana near Treporti. He did not own the *valle* but rented it and worked it for his own profit. There is a lot of work involved in running a *valle* properly and although my grandfather had his three brothers working with him, he usually had to take on extra men and that was what led to disaster. These men used to drag for fish on their own account on the nights when my grandfather and his brothers were not working (because, of course, you don't drag every night) and so the stock of fish diminished and very little profit came in to my grandfather. Soon, *purtroppo*, he found himself penniless. You cannot trust anybody, you know, outside your own family. Besides the *valle*, my grandfather had about thirty acres of land. There again he was not the owner, only the tenant. These same fields which I work now were part of the land he had. He and his brothers made a good living when they had both the *valle* and these fields. It was more than enough to keep all four families. Then the brothers broke up. You know how families are. The brothers disagreed. quarrelled with one another, decided to go their own ways. At the same time the families were growing in size, more children arriving all the time, until it became difficult to have enough to go round and this led to further arguments about dividing the crops and the profits they got from them. The next generation divided up the land held by my grandfather and his brothers. You cannot really call it an inheritance which was divided because we had never owned the land. We had always been tenants, never owners. We were not *mezzadri*. We did not have to share our harvest with a proprietor or agree with him what crops should be planted or how to market them. We paid a rent every year and were free to do what we liked with the land. So we were better off than the *mezzadri*. We are still tenants, those of us who have remained on the land. All this land round here belongs — always has belonged — to the Venice *Comune* (Municipality) which lets it out to various families. My family have been tenants here for, oh, at least two hundred years, tenants, tenants all the time. For at least two hundred years my old ancestors have lived in this house and worked this land, and it still does not belong to us.

Now, this big old house is where I was born. It was my grandfather's house. This house and the one on the other side of the yard are divided up between the children and grandchildren of my grandfather and his three brothers. My grandfather was the eldest and all but one of my brothers have left the land and have given us their rights in the house and the land. So, as a result, we have a little more room than the other families who live here. This house, especially all divided up into bits between people who are not very closely related any more and who do not always want to live so close to one another, who have different ideas about proper behaviour and what sort of people they want their children to become, this house, as I was saying, is not adapted to the standard of living today.

Now the *comune* is thinking of selling the freehold of this land and I may have the chance to buy the parts I have been working all my life. We will see. Prices are so high these days. In any case I could not be turned out. The law does not allow that, these days. I could continue as a tenant but I do not know whether that would be a success. It would depend on what sort of person the new owner turned out to be.

My father worked this land just as we do. His share of the land was 10,000 square metres, that is to say one hectare (2.70 acres). Now my brother (he lives next door here, you have met him) and I have 5,000 square metres each. It is not enough to keep a family. Even 10,000 square metres was not enough in my father's day. My father was a good *contadino* (peasant), very skilful in cultivating the land, but even he could not manage to feed us all on 10,000 square metres. We all had to go out to work as soon as we could and we helped him on the land in our spare time. We worked here in the evenings and sometimes in the mornings, depending on what our work was, and always on Sundays. I have worked hard all my life and so has my wife, Mistica, and my children. Since I went to work at the Cà S. Tomà in Torcello, ten or twelve years ago now, I have worked twenty days in the month for a salary and the rest of the time I work here on my own behalf. I work every minute of daylight when I get back from Torcello and still on Sundays. My wife and I have always worked every minute we could. We used to get some help from brothers and sisters and their wives and husbands, and we still do, but we do not have to ask them for so much now that the girls are growing up and have left school. Antonietta is seventeen now and Eufemia fifteen and they are a great help. My boy Sergio cannot help very much yet because he is only ten. You know how hard Mistica and I have worked because you have known us for so long and you know how heavy the work is.

As I said, we could not live off the land even in my father's time, but things became really difficult after he died. My mother had a very hard time bringing us all up properly. When my father died I was only four and I was the next to youngest of nine children. My eldest brother was sixteen at the time and went off to work in a glass factory in Murano. He used to bring home 500 lire a week and we were very glad to see it. That must have been in 1943. The other children went out to work as soon as they could and soon there were several little wage packets coming in every week. Apart from my fourth brother, who shares the land with me here, the rest have all left the land. My eldest brother later became a boatman. He drives one of those big *mototopi* which carry freight all over the lagoon. My next brother became a mason. He is one of the men who look after the basilica of St. Mark's and you have often seen him there. My third brother left home soon after my father died and was taken in charge by the Church as he intended to become a priest. He was a deacon for a time and was in charge of a hostel in Paris for Italian working men, but then he decided not to become a priest and settled in Rome. Except for this brother, we all live here near one another in Treporti. We are all married and all have families, all five brothers and four sisters. It was a fine time when we all started to grow up and get married. We had to keep dividing our share of the house to make room for everybody! But gradually the other brothers moved away, one to Rome and two to their own houses which they built near here, and the sisters, of course, went to their husbands' houses, so my brother and I who stayed here have been quite well off really.

When we were children we did not do much playing. Con-

170

ditions in the family were too difficult. I went to school up to the third year of the primary level and then, my goodness, I had to start work to help the family have enough bread to eat. Things were much harder in those days than they are today. I worked on our land, growing crops to sell or else helping my uncles with their land in return for the help they gave us. So I did not work for wages in those days. My uncles gave us a great deal of help because, of course, there were a lot of things we were not strong enough to do or which we had not yet learnt how to do. For instance, my uncles used to prune our vines because we did not know how and they killed our pigs for us and taught us how to make *salami* of various kinds. And, as I said, we used to work on their land, doing whatever we were capable of doing, in exchange. And my brothers and sisters and I still help one another as we each have become specialists at one thing or another in our lives and on the land. Life would be very difficult without one's brothers and sisters.

Sometimes on a Sunday when I was little, not always but sometimes, when we were lucky, we had enough money left over at the end of the week to buy a few toffees. Then we used to be so happy! My mother used to hand them out to us here in this room. Just one or two for each of us. This room has always been our kitchen and the room where we lived. We slept in another room over in the other house across the yard. But this is where we always lived.

So I began to work on the land at the age of eleven, doing what I could, what I knew how to do and what I had the strength for *in somma*. Then I was employed by a contractor and did various land jobs for him. For instance, I worked for six months in Venice in the gardens of S. Giorgio Maggiore when the Cini Foundation was being set up. I planted most of those hedges in the open-air theatre there. Then I worked for another contractor who used to look after the vineyards which the Armenian fathers, the ones who have the monastery on the island of S. Lazzaro near the Lido, possess in this part of the lagoon. They own fine vineyards here in Treporti and further along in Lio Piccolo.

I have also worked as a fisherman. When my brothers and I divided up the tenancy I mostly worked my own bit, which

171

was quite small, until it was finally agreed that we two who had stayed on the land should have the whole of my father's share between us. But even that was not enough to keep a family. It was just 5,000 square metres, as I said. On this land I mostly grew greenstuffs, salads of all kinds, beans, peas and so on for market. But to make ends meet I used to work in the *valli* during the months of September, October and November (what we call the *tempo di fraiima*), and even to within two or three days of Christmas if the weather was mild. During this time the fish in the *valli* are caught in a drag-net and sent to market. I worked in all for seven seasons of *fraiima* in privately owned *valli*. And, would you believe it, I was mostly working in my grandfather's old *valli*, the ones he had to give up because his hired help stole so much from him. And now I was hired help myself in the same *valli*.

The work in the *valli* goes like this. There is work to do all the year round, even if the actual taking of the fish is mostly restricted to the months of the *fraiima*. In April, for instance, the *novelami*, the tiny little fish brought in by lagoon fishermen, have to be released into the *valli* to grow. Then, when the fishing actually starts, those fish that are still not big enough for market are turned into special enclosures until they do get big enough. Usually they stay in these enclosures during the winter months and that is why they are mostly filled with sweet water. Sea-water does not freeze easily and fish fear nothing so much as cold, rough water in shallow places. But sweet water freezes and the fish are quite safe under ice. You can begin fishing before the proper *tempo di fraiima* begins. But whenever you begin you have to work at night. In July and August fish eat and get fat, but if you fish them during the day when they are feeding they taste muddy and are not very nice. So usually the fish are taken at night when they have stopped feeding. The fish start feeding again when day breaks so you can count on some hours between midnight and one o'clock when you begin fishing and about three or four o'clock when you have to stop.

In July and August we also get these tremendous storms at night, cloudbursts when the rain comes down in sheets all over the lagoon. Then, if you are out in the *valli* you will see the fish sticking their heads up out of the water to drink

172

because the rain, of course, is sweet water. You see them all over the place pushing up their heads and making little circles of ripples and disappearing, and then popping up to drink some more. You also have to fish when the tide is up because when it goes out the water becomes very shallow in the *valli* and the fish hide in the mud at the bottom and are impossible to catch. They also hide during the cold weather and protect themselves from the cold in the mud at the bottom of the lagoon. In any case, you do not usually fish in winter because they do not feed then, as the plants they live on have withered away and the fish become thin and bony. In the summer, on the other hand, they live in the shallow parts where they find more to eat. So these *pesce di rio* (fish in the channels) are taken at night and that is why you see all those boats with bright lights working along the deeper channels in the *valli*. Fishing with *forcine* (tridents) is also done at night but that is quite a different story, quite another method. You have two men in a *sandalo*, the one in the prow standing over the lamp spears the fish with his *forcina* and the other manoeuvres the boat. Then there is fishing *a sorbera* which can be done by one man but is quicker when there are two or three. One rows, and the others pay out the net and later draw it in. In this sort of fishing you beat the water with an oar to scare the fish into the net. These kinds of fishing are done in the lagoon.

Now fishing in the *valli, nei fondali* or *nei buoi* as we say, is quite different. You need a team of ten to twelve men. Here you have big, heavy nets which have to be paid out evenly on either side of a long thin *valle* or round the edge of a pond-like one. You have four or five men on the banks at each end of the net and one or two in a boat in the middle to keep the net upright. You have to manage the net carefully so that it scrapes along the bottom and yet never goes below the surface. The nets are, of course, weighted with lead to keep them on the bottom and the top side is floated with corks to make sure it stays on the surface. If you leave gaps below or above the fish will slip through or jump over. The men on the sides haul the net along, and very heavy work it is too, until the two teams meet either at the end of an oblong enclosure or at some point on the bank of a round one. The

173

teams have to be very careful to draw first on the lower rope which is tied to the *piombo* (leaded side) and then on the *suro* (cork) to make sure that the net remains perpendicular. And then you haul in hand over hand, *piombo, suro, piombo, suro*, until the net is quite closed and you can begin tipping the fish out into baskets. The man drawing the *piombo* has the hardest work, the *suro* is much lighter because of the cork and because all the fish are crowded together down at the bottom, not at the top. The *suro* man really only has to make sure that he keeps pace with the *piombo* team, that is to say slightly behind so that there is a drag which helps to keep the net upright, otherwise it would fold over and the fish go off. For some reason the *piombo* man was always me. Maybe because I was young. They always give them the really hard jobs.

I learnt modern methods of cultivating my land by going to lectures and demonstrations organised by the farmers' association I belong to. They also bring out a useful newsheet and leaflets and booklets which I get and study. Until about five years ago specialists used to come round about twice a month to demonstrate various skills, for instance, the correct way of pruning. Twenty or so of us used to meet in .an orchard and we would spend the afternoon watching the expert pruning and listen to him explaining the reasons why he pruned the way he did. Another time we would meet in a vineyard and again the expert would prune rows of vines and explain his methods and answer all our questions. My English *padrona* at the Cà' S. Tomà said that I was the best pruner she had ever met. She used to say that I was a specialist. You could not say that I had studied pruning. No. But I had watched experts and found out why they pruned in that particular way and tried to put their methods into practice. I followed the example of the specialists, that is what I did and they made the reasons clear to me. They were very precise. They would say: "Leave this bud, take the second one here, cut off this because it crosses that stronger branch." You need to see and have the reasons explained once or twice and then you can do it quite well yourself. It is a matter of experience rather than study.

My *padrona* also said that I was an expert at growing

artichokes. But before I started working at the Cà' S. Tomà I had never grown a single one. Here in Treporti the land is not suitable for artichokes so we never grow any. Here we have a light, sandy soil. In Torcello it is heavier, almost a clay, as you see, when it rains. It sticks to everything and in the hot weather it cracks. Really, it is silt brought down by the rivers which, in the old days, used to run into the lagoon. Now they have all been deflected, of course, as part of the old Republic's flood controls. The soil in Torcello is extremely fertile but even there some things flourish better than others. Artichokes and vines grow exceedingly well. Asparagus, on the other hand, becomes weak and stringy and is practically a failure. In Treporti, however, it grows like a weed, both the fat white kind and the tasty thin green kind. So one has to know the land to plant crops which are suited to the conditions and will grow vigorously.

The way I learnt about growing artichokes in Torcello was by watching the neighbours to see what they were doing and by trying to think out the reasons why they did it, and soon I was growing better stuff than they were. Better crops than most native-born Torcellani *contadini* could raise. I did not see why growing artichokes should create great difficulties and indeed I did not find it difficult, *ecco*. The artichoke plants which I put in when I first went to work there are beginning to die. This is not because the plants themselves are too old or not able to produce more artichokes but because, as you know very well, the soil gets exhausted if it has only one crop growing on it for eight, nine or ten years. Then the soil needs attention. That is to say, that it has to be dug deep with the under layer put on top and vice versa and then the plants grow again vigorously. A plant which has been feeding off the top layer for ten years has naturally drawn all the good out of it. And the whole art of cultivation lies in giving plants a constant supply of the food they need. For the soil to give it, it must be turned. An artichoke plant can last up to fifteen years but after ten years you get less return in fruit (an artichoke is really a flower bud and not a fruit, however) and you get more losses from frost and so on among the old, less vigorous plants.

You cannot expect the soil to provide everything an artichoke needs to give a good crop. You have to give fertiliser or, better still, manure if you can get it. In the lagoon nowadays there are very few cows and no horses. The best and richest manure is fowl manure. In the first years at the Cà' S. Tomà we always managed to get it but now it is hard to find and expensive so we have had to take to fertilisers.

Artichokes should be given manure or fertiliser in November at the time when the plantation is being cleaned up for the winter. At the Cà' S. Tomà we had rows of artichokes between the vines and so the whole place was cleaned up and put to bed for the winter in one go. Very convenient and labour-saving that was. As far as the artichokes were concerned one first scattered manure round the plant, then one hoed it in and made a mound of soil about a foot high on the northern side of the plant, bending the plant over a bit towards the south. This heap of soil protects the plant from the *bora*, which is our cold north wind, and also prevents rain getting into the heart of the plant and freezing there if the weather is severe. It also serves to turn the plant towards the warmth of the sun when the growing season starts in the spring.

At about the end of March the new season's work starts, on St. Joseph's Day, that is to say March 19, provided that the cold weather has ended. The first job is to remove the mounds which were made in November. This you do with a spade and spread the earth around, and then you give another little scattering of manure to encourage the plant a bit. As soon as the *figli* (side-shoots, literally children) grow about a foot high, they have to be pulled out to leave a strong main stem. People eat the white stems of the *figli* as a vegetable. They are tender and have a delicate artichoke taste, and are welcome because they come after a long winter with little variety of greenstuff. When you tidy the plant for the winter you usually have to pull out some *figli* but nobody is very interested in them then after the good crops of the summer and autumn.

Round about April 25, and provided the temperature is reasonable, the artichokes begin to form. Then you pick the *castranga*, the first-born, the bud that grows at the tip of the main stem of the plant. Then, depending on the mildness of

176

the season and the vigour of the plant, you can hope to pick three or four *primi bottoli*, though I have known bad years when there have only been two and propitious years when I have seen as many as five on a plant. So the *primo bottolo* is the second-born. At the base of each leaf of the *primo bottolo* branch is the bud of the next series. This is what we call the *carciofo* and it is the main crop. The ones that come before are really *primeurs*. Then, if you are lucky with the weather and get good rain, particularly at night, because artichokes need rain, a lot of rain, to become fat and tender, you can expect a good crop. The number of *carciofi* you can hope for depends on the health and vigour of the plant. There are phenomenal plants and disappointing plants and one never quite knows why. At the Cà S. Tomà I have picked twenty-five *carciofi* from a single plant. I mean twenty-five at one cutting. Three or four days later I would come back and cut another twenty-five. Now, I am not inventing this. I have got a witness. You remember my cousin Maria who used to help me with the harvesting? Well, she will tell you that we used to take twenty-five at each cutting from a great many plants. This is a phenomenon. You do not usually get so many. The soil of Torcello is certainly a paradise for *carciofi*. The average from a plant runs, I suppose, from thirty-five to fifty, depending on the quality of the plants. Let us say an average of forty. That is about right. Even to get that you must have rain. No *carciofi* without rain. The end of the season is June 29, when you cut the last *fondi* (large artichokes where only the heart is eaten). By that time the choke of the artichoke is beginning to blossom out into that gorgeous blue flower. If you see a lot of those blue flowers in a plantation it means either that the season was dry and therefore bad, or else that the grower did not know how to harvest his crop.

In the vineyard at Cà S. Tomà we grew four types of vine. Two red, Merlot and Raboso, and two white, Verduzzo and Tokai. The Merlot did best, then the Raboso which, however, never gave a really first-class crop, good but nothing phenomenal, you understand. The Verduzzo was middling and the Tokai was terrible — a real disaster. It demanded more attention than all the others put together. I had to spray it twice as often and it only gave a few *quintali* (one *quintale* = 220 lbs). A real waste of time it was and finally I persuaded my *padrona* to graft the Tokai stocks with a more productive local white grape. Not all the grafts caught, of course, but it was better than having that beastly, troublesome Tokai. Oh, I did hate that Tokai.

Apart from caring for the vines, one has to make sure that all the *pali* which carry the wires supporting the vines are in good order. With the vigorous plants putting out long branches fifteen to twenty feet long with a great weight of leaves and later fruit, hundredweights, tons of fruit, these *pali* had to be strong. Besides that, the wall of leaves used to get thoroughly buffeted by winds during the storms we get here in the summer. So, for this reason too, the *pali* had to be strong. We had concrete *pali* spaced out along each row and wooden *pali* in between. These wooden *pali* had to be replaced from time to time when they became weak. In some years we had to order as many as a hundred new *pali*, and I used to go and pick them out myself to be sure that the wood was sound and the *palo* straight and solid. Chestnut is the best. It is a good wood which stands up well to this heavy work. You have to be careful about the *pali*. Those which have grown on southern slopes are much stronger and more resistant than those which have matured on northern slopes. These do not get enough sun and altogether too much water to make a sound, solid timber. The wood is tender and weak if it grows too much in the shade.

Then there is the pruning to do, both of the vines and the fruit trees. At the Cà' S. Tomà we had mostly peaches, plums and pears (but they did not do very well) and other trees such as apricots, cherries, quince and so on, just for the house. Not enough attention is paid nowadays to the period when pruning should be done. The moon certainly has an influence. *Però*, pruning should be done when the moon is waning. To give you an example: you know that one uses the *stroppe* (prunings) of the vines to tie up the plants? Well, if these *stroppe* have been cut when the moon was waxing you will find that, out of every hundred, thirty will be good and seventy will break. This is a bit of a mystery, but there you are. I have often noticed it. So you are put to the trouble of

178

soaking all those wands for nothing if they break when you use them to tie up the vines. You also see the influence of the moon in sowing seeds, particularly salads like lettuce or *radicchio* (a salad with pinkish leaves and a strong tapered root, a speciality of Treviso and Castelfranco near Venice). It is well known that if you plant these during a waxing moon, half of them will bolt before they are fully grown. We are always careful to note the moon and the tide when we sow these salads. Both should be decreasing. The moon and the tide should accompany one another. It is the same with killing a pig. If you slaughter a pig at home you will find that the *salami* does not turn out as well. You notice a difference. You notice it particularly if you have slaughtered a boar, it makes less difference with a hog, but with a boar, my goodness, if you have slaughtered at the wrong moment, the *salami* smells high, it stinks. It has partly to do with being the meat of a boar, which is always stronger, but it also has to do with the moon.

I learnt how to sell market produce by watching other people at Venice market, at Rialto. I soon saw that properly prepared, neatly packed and well-presented produce sold first and at good prices. I learnt that order paid. It is just the same with human beings. It is bad enough not to be beautiful without being untidy and grubby as well. Even an ugly chap is acceptable if he is clean and neat, and so it is with everything. At market the neatness and order of a box of produce, whether artichokes or peaches, makes an immediate impression. Also, when you see that there is a mad rush to buy something you should hold off. You should not sell immediately, because it usually means that there is a shortage of that particular produce that morning. So the price is sure to rise and that is the moment to sell. You may get 20 lire more and that will be worth having. On the other hand, if the buying is slack you have to go along with the price offered even if you think it is too low. Otherwise you will have all your produce left on your hands and then what will you do? Slow buying usually means that there was too much of that produce the day before and that everybody has stocked up, or else that there has been a glut and people are tired of seeing it. It is all a matter of looking round and watching out and remembering what happened last time. Experience, that is what it is. There are no professional sellers in a market as far as I can see — just everybody doing the best they can for themselves.

Here at home we grow as much as we can for the house. We prefer good, pure, simple food that has not been tampered with. Look what they do to meat these days. Filling animals full of chemicals! And the wine! Just one glass gives you a headache. We make our own wine out of grapes and nothing else. It is not like some of the wine you buy which is full of various powders and chemicals. I drink our wine with pleasure. I can take two or three glasses and feel fine whereas, years ago, when I still used to drink bought wine I used to feel heavy and out of sorts on just one glass. It must have been adulterated. So, I do not really trust products made by other people. I like to eat and drink real, genuine things. I like to make as much of our food myself as I possibly can. Then I know what goes into it, whether it is wine or *salami.* Now, in the new house we have got a deep-freeze and will be able to have a better, more varied diet of our own growing during the winter months. We have chickens and rabbits too, so we do not have to depend too much on the shops.

We raise a few pigs and kill one occasionally. I do not know how but I have a brother who does and he comes in to do it and, of course, he shares the meat. Most of us round here keep pigs. There are strict sanitary regulations. You have to take the liver to a local butcher here who keeps them all in his cold room to await the weekly visit of the veterinary inspector. If there is anything wrong with the liver the whole carcase is confiscated. We make a lot of *salami* and if you do it properly they remain good for two years. We make all kinds but particularly one which we call *sorpressa,* which keeps very well. Generally, the larger a sausage is, the better it keeps. They need care. They must be kept in the cool and this is not always easy in hot weather. They must be cool but not, however, in a draught. Keeping them in a refrigerator is not ideal. They will keep very well for a month or two but for longer conservation they should not be in a refrigerator. They keep better, longer, just in a cool place.

You have to know how to make *salami,* particularly if you intend to keep them for a long time. You must know exactly how much salt and spices to put in, though this depends on personal taste. For instance, one will put in $4\frac{1}{2}$% of salt, another only $3\frac{1}{2}$%. That is about the safe minimum for long keeping.

We now have good water piped from the mainland across the lagoon. The main pipeline rises out of the lagoon at the Casa Bianca where the Treporti *vaporetto* stop is. We had tremendous trouble getting the water. Before we got it we had an artesian well here. All of us families clubbed together to pay a contractor to sink it for us and it gave quite good water. It tasted a little rusty because of the pipes we had used, but it was perfectly healthy and much better than the shallow well we had before which was brackish. We were terribly pleased when we heard that the main pipeline was to run along the road from Casa Bianca to Treporti and soon we saw a large depot of lengths of pipe being stacked up by the road. We were not pleased, however, when the *Comune* of Venice told us that the water was not for us but only for the tourist centres along the sea-shore. Imagine that! All that water just for two months of the tourist season and leaving us without any water for twelve months of the year. We were not going to have that! Now we know that this is not an important road, but it is quite long. It starts at the bridge by the cemetery and runs the whole length of the island of Saccagnana and it serves a number of families. In all, there must be a thousand, fifteen hundred or even more people living along the road and the fields round about.

So we had a meeting to decide what to do. And we all agreed to act the following Sunday. When Sunday morning came we all turned out with whatever transport we could get hold of, trucks, vans, cars, tractors, and we carried off all the pipes stacked up in the depot. Every single pipe! We distributed them among ourselves and hid them wherever we could, in farmyards and buildings and under haystacks. The next day the *carabinieri* came round looking about and asking questions. "Pipes?" we said, "no, we haven't seen any pipes. What sort of pipes would it be that you are looking for?" You should have seen their faces! Naturally, they knew

181

what had happened. There were too many of us involved to keep that secret, but they could not arrest us all, not every single householder. So the *Comune* had to agree to bring a branch line down this road to supply all the houses on Saccagnana. Then, mysteriously, the next Sunday all the pipes reappeared neatly stacked where they had been before. We all had a good laugh.

But that was not the end. When the branch pipeline got as far as this house the *Comune* and the contractor stopped work. Now, further along the road there are other families. I know the road is not made up properly, it is really only an old-fashioned country dirt-track, but it was not fair after what had been agreed. Now, the people along there had taken their share in hauling off and hiding the pipes and we could not leave them in the lurch. We stick together in this part of the world. It was a case of all or none. Solidarity, that is what it was. This time it was mostly the women who decided what to do because it was during the week and most of the men were at work. But the men who were free took part, naturally. They all went off carrying whatever they could that could make a barricade, old chairs, branches of trees, uprooted bushes, and they barred the main road which runs from Jesolo to Punta Sabbioni, where the car ferry leaves for Venice. They barred it at the Cà' Savio crossroads. And then they all sat down, women and children all over the crossroads. Hundreds of them, there were! They had taken their lunch and things to drink and the *carabinieri* were at their wits end. It would have taken an army corps to move that lot. On each side of the crossroads there grew an enormous queue of cars stretching for kilometres on either side of the crossroads, full of angry tourists, and, you know, those Germans get angry rather easily. Some missed their boat to Venice and others wanted to get back to their caravans to feed the children. And our women just sat chatting and eating their lunch and the children had a lovely time playing about, and the traffic lights kept changing and the queue of cars kept hooting. After nearly an hour of this the *Comune* had to send a man to promise that they would keep their word and everybody on Saccagnana would get piped water. Mistica here got her photograph into the newspaper along with the girls. Sergio was too young to go. He was only three at the time.

Very soon now we will have a house of our own, at a cost of twenty years of saving and sacrifices. But it will be our own place, worth it all. As I told you, I have 5,000 square metres of land here rented from the *Comune* and also a part of the house. But we can never be *padroni* here and any improvements we make belong to the *Comune* and not to us. So naturally we did not want to spend money here putting in bathrooms and a modern kitchen to make ourselves comfortable at what would be a benefit to somebody else in the long run. It would be throwing money in the air. So we decided to make the effort of buying a place of our own and the long years of sacrifice which we knew it would entail. At first we could only put aside 100,000 lire a year. The lire was worth more in those days but even then it was little enough. Later we could put aside more and now that the girls are working with us we can grow more and so sell more and put aside more. We have spent a pile of money on that place! Everything has become so expensive in these last few years. If we could have built it ten years ago we would have paid about half what we have had to spend. I like to do everything properly and legally and so I applied for planning permission and a building licence, and you would not believe the delay that involved us in. In the meantime costs were going up every day. Just at present you have to pay a skilled mason three times what he got three years ago. We have done as much as we could ourselves or through family contacts, but, nonetheless, building a house is a technical business and you have to have a proper builder who knows his job. You cannot do everything yourself.

First we bought the land. We bought 5,000 square metres, as much as I rent here. That in itself presented a problem. We did not want the land to stand idle. I was working five days a week at the Cà' S. Tomà. The children were too young to help much. So we had double the land to work between Mistica nearly full-time and me two days a week and in the evenings. It is a lot of work to keep 10,000 square metres properly and intensively cultivated, not to speak of harvesting, packing and marketing. My goodness, how we have worked during these last few years. As you see, we are not very fat. We eat well but we work too hard to get fat. Nowadays we take a good crop from the land, particularly since we started to protect the plants with these plastic structures. They are expensive to build but I do it myself with the help of my brothers. The plastic is fragile and has to be protected with these tough nets because we are in a hail belt here and the nets help to break the force of the hailstones. The warm air coming in from the sea meets the cold air from the land just up above us and we get frightful hailstorms. Before we had these plastic sheds I have lost a whole crop of tomatoes in ten minutes. Now, at the Cà' S. Tomà, which is only five kilometres away, I have never seen a hailstorm, not the kind we get here. Torcello is protected by the warm air of the lagoon. These nets make more expense but, *in somma*, it is worth it if you can save a crop.

We cultivated the new land for three years before we had put aside enough money to think of starting to build. I suppose we can now say that we have just about finished. We have not yet bought the boiler for the central heating and you really must have central heating in this damp place. But we should be able to move in within the year.

The living part of the house is upstairs. It has a good living-room and a big kitchen with a balcony, a hall, three bedrooms and a bathroom. Downstairs is a big *magazzino* for storing the tractor and all the other tools and equipment, and also the boxes of produce ready to be collected for market. This takes up about half the space, and the rest perhaps one day could be turned into a little house for one of the children when they get married. We have piped water and electricity and our own soakaway sewage plant. Like everybody else in these parts we cook with bottled gas. It is very practical.

Yes, of course, we are pleased about the house, very happy. We are relieved too because I do not think that either of us could have gone on working as hard as we have for very much longer. Both Mistica and I are just about done. The girls have been wonderful. They both have half-time jobs now and they help us the rest of the time. But naturally the main weight has fallen on Mistica and me. We have been working almost day and night for years. We have not had a day off for years, just a few hours here and there for family occasions. In the summer we always try to take the children to the beach and get a bit of rest ourselves. We go to the beach here at Treporti. It is one of the best and is where all the people from here and Burano go. You don't get many tourists there. It is mostly local people but you never know when someone is going to run up a huge caravan site just in your favourite spot. Still, I cannot complain, it is the tourists who eat my produce.'

4 Santa Cristina—A Waste Land

Santa Cristina lies beyond Torcello — first by the S. Antonio canal past the island of S. Ariana, where the bones from the Venice graveyard used to be dumped when the brief period of occupancy was up, on past La Cura till it joins the S. Lorenzo canal and then off north by a side canal to the island. It is surrounded by *palude* and just to the south-east lie the old salt pans of S. Felice and further east the *valli* where fish are bred and caught for market.

Like so many of the little islands in this part of the lagoon, Santa Cristina was occupied by a convent. In the ninth century the doge Vitale Falier gave the island of S. Murco to the Benedictines who built a convent. In 1325 the body of Santa Cristina, the Virgin of Tyre, was transported to the island from Constantinople which from that date took her name. Then followed years of the vicissitudes which pursued so many of these lagoon foundations. In 1340 lack of sweet water drove the nuns away to Venice but when the crisis was past they returned with great pomp and ceremony. In 1452 the community had dwindled to one nun, the abbess Philippa

Condulmer, who was allowed to transfer to the convent of S. Antonio which then existed in Torcello. At that time the body of Santa Cristina was taken to S. Francesco della Vigna in Venice where it still is. This signalled the permanent decay and gradual disappearance of the convent except for fragments incorporated here and there into the buildings used to house the *contadini* who tilled the fields and the fishermen who tended the *valli*.

These *valli* were a source of wealth for many generations. They were also rich shooting grounds, particularly for wild duck which came in to feed from the sea. Some of them have been in the same ownership for centuries. Beyond Santa Cristina to the east lie the vast areas set aside to provide the reigning doge with enough duck to produce five for the head of each patrician family when he came to offer his Christmas greetings. Nowadays the duck shooting has greatly fallen off. They are scarcer and the constant noise of outboard motors even in remote stretches of the lagoon is making them shyer still.

The *valli* round Santa Cristina ceased to be worked after the last war because they no longer paid, and soon after the last of the population left the island. Now it has been bought as a summer residence. The main house has been rebuilt, higher than is usual in the lagoon, and some people in Burano call it the block of flats. It is certainly not a mannerly building, seeking to fit in with the landscape, but at least it has saved the island from crumbling into the lagoon. Santa Cristina has been properly embanked now at the cost of the owner, and the *valli* have been restored and, some say, enlarged.

The tiny village community died when the island was abandoned in 1948. Now it is a rich man's toy but at least it still exists, unlike the many islands which have been gradually washed away by the tides. Socially, it is a waste land.

An Old Lady Looks Back

'It takes an hour to get to Santa Cristina from Burano or Torcello. Oh, by rowing boat, *certo*, by rowing boat! With an outboard motor it would take maybe a quarter of an hour, maybe less, but we did not have any outboard motors in those days.

I first went to live in Santa Cristina after the 1915-1918 war. I was about twelve then. We lived here in Torcello when I was small and we all went to school in the church because there wasn't a proper school-house here then. They made one later but when they had to close it because the schoolmistress retired and there were only two or three children left, the *locanda* took over the building. Cipriani's *locanda,* of course. I did three years' schooling there and then we went to Milan for a year and then back to Torcello for another year and then we went to live in Santa Cristina. I stayed there till I was married and then I came back to Torcello!

Santa Cristina was a beautiful place, *stupendo.* When I first went to live there we were sixty-one persons in all but later we were only thirty-six or thirty-seven. The houses were old but good. There were two of them but later we made another little house, a *carivetta,* and then there was a house for each of the three families. The children, particularly the little children, had a lovely life. We used to work hard helping in the fields and the vineyards. Of course the children did not get any schooling. *Dio mio* it was too far away. I was very lucky that way. I had finished before we went there.

It was a big island about half the size of Torcello. We had more than thirty fields. We grew everything: asparagus, the fat white ones and those little thin green *asparagetti* which taste so good, fruit of all kinds, apples, pears, peaches, strawberries, cherries, grapes and maize to make *polenta.* We grew enough to feed us all the year. We ate *polenta* every day, *certo.*

At first we had to go and get water from Lio Piccolo. Every day the boat had to go and, of course, with all those people and the animals we needed a lot of water and had to be very careful with it when we did get it. It was about as far as Torcello and took about an hour's rowing each way. The boats went down towards the canal di San Lorenzo, where there was an old church long ago (it has now disappeared, just a hump on a *barena)* and then off to the left to the canal di San Felice where the old salt pans are, to Lio Piccolo. Then the owners of the land, our *padroni* (because we were a *mezzadria* like everybody else in those days) dug us an artesian well, a *fontana* as we say. It gave good, pure water. We had a lot of animals — eighteen or twenty cows — so we needed water. We did not sell milk, we were too far away and in any case people drank very little milk in those days,

but we made our own cheese. It hadn't got a name, we just called it *formaggio casalinga* (home-made cheese). It was good and became hard and kept well. We did not sell it out-side the island but it all got used up among the households on Santa Cristina. We also had fish, mostly from the *fosse* (enclosures where fish are bred, sometimes in deep canals round higher land, sometimes with staked enclosures in the shallower parts of the open lagoon). But the fish were mostly sent away to market. We lived very well. We didn't eat much fish as I have said but we did not lack for food of every kind, poultry, pigs (we killed four or five a year), fruit, vegetables, and *polenta*. We ate a lot of *polenta*.

We never went to Venice. The only time I ever went to Venice from Santa Cristina was to be blessed at the church of the Madonna della Salute there. That was a great day, very exciting and very long, all in a rowing boat! We had to come in to Burano or Torcello to mass. We belonged to the parish of Torcello but some of us used to go to Burano, maybe because there was more life there after our quiet ways. The older women seldom came to mass. The young women used to come regularly and afterwards we sometimes went off to amuse ourselves. Life has changed in all sorts of ways. When one is old one likes one's old ways. I do not want to go off any more to amuse myself. I like to stay quiet and do things about the house. But in those days we used to take the boats out and somebody played the accordion and sometimes we did not get back till midnight.

When one of us got married a really good accordion player would come over from Burano and eating, drinking and dancing went on for a week. What a time we used to have! When I got married (it was a double wedding, my cousin and I got married on the same day) we didn't get up from table for two days. We had chicken and rice and pork and fish and all good genuine food which we had produced ourselves. Our own good wine too.

Now nobody lives on Santa Cristina. That life has all gone. They tell me there are still fish-farms but that the fields are water-logged and not cultivated any more. They have been working on and off for about ten years, reinforcing the banks to keep the *acqua alta* out, and have rebuilt the house. They have been spending millions. We will see what happens. It was the great flood of 1936 which did the most damage. Before that in Santa Cristina and here in Torcello one of the great crops was peaches. They were a special kind which travelled well so they could be picked when they were nearly ripe, not green like the modern ones you buy in shops, but almost ripe so that they tasted of something. A lot were sent to markets in other countries. Then came the 1936 floods and all the trees died and now the trees do not last. They produce for a few years and then they get worm and die. But vines do well. In Santa Cristina the wine was so strong you had to put water into it. The soil was good for vines there and then with all those animals we had all the manure we needed. But nobody lives there now. Nobody wants to live so far away. Where have all those people gone, I wonder? To the *terraferma* I suppose or to Treporti or Cavallino.'

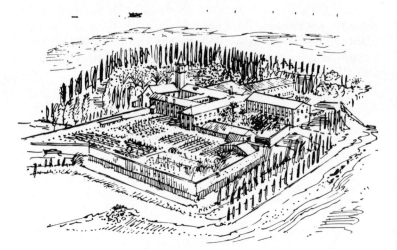

5 San Francesco del Deserto
—An Oasis

If Burano has found a way to re-affirm its sense of community and Torcello has been diminished almost to a nonsociety by the pressures of the twentieth century, San Francesco del Deserto has gently pursued the vocation for which it was founded. It has not sought to compete with the world. It continues as an oasis of peace on earth.

This tiny island lies some half-mile to the south of Burano and is approached by a narrow canal winding through the shallows. The first impression is one of a mass of cypresses from which rises the *campanile* of the little church. The island is so quiet it seems deserted and the sound of the bell one has rung jangles shockingly loud. Then there is the slip-slop of sandalled feet, the door is flung wide and one is gently and kindly welcomed by one of the community of ten who now live and work there. The impression of tranquillity, order and kindliness grows as one is shown the old church, the cell of St. Francis and the cloister gay with geraniums in pots. Then one is led into the garden with cypresses and lime trees and oleanders and peacocks and bantams and doves and pheasants and shown the tree where the owl used to live. There is a walk along the old bank lined with cypresses and a belvedere looking over to Burano with its leaning *campanile*. Now the bank is doubled by a second bank to ensure that no flood waters enter the island and this bank too has been planted with cypresses still young and pencil-thin.

In 1220 St. Francis landed in Torcello from a Venetian ship on his return from a missionary journey to Palestine and Egypt and came to the *Isola delle Due Vigne* where he found a great multitude of birds singing in the trees, and said to his companions: 'Since our brothers the birds are singing the praises of their Creator, let us also go amongst them to praise the Lord', and to the birds he said: 'Brother birds, cease your song until we have ended our praises', and the birds were silent until the end of the mass when, at a word from the Saint, they took up there song again. St. Francis founded a hermitage on the island and, indeed, traces of an ancient cell have recently been found there. Tradition maintains that St. Francis when he landed on the island stuck his pilgrim's staff into the ground and that it grew into the gigantic tree which died in 1701. The brothers still show visitors the partially fossilised trunk.

In 1228 St Francis was canonised and the Venetian patrician, Jacopo Michiel, to whom the island belonged, gave it to the order in perpetuity in 1233. This marks the start of a long connection between the island on the one hand and Venetian nobility and the Patriarchate of Venice on the other. Their protection and generosity led to the construction of the church and monastery buildings and the survival of the monastery through many difficult times. From the foundation of the monastery the island was known as San Francesco.

At this time many convents and monasteries were being founded in islands in the lagoon and during the thirteenth and fourteenth centuries all of them suffered from changes in movements of the water and in the levels it attained. The increase in the stagnant areas of the marshes brought mosquitoes and malaria, and sudden rises in water levels and the capriciousness of the tides undermined land masses and the foundations of buildings. From 1400 onwards a number of churches and convents disappeared entirely, such as S. Lorenzo and S. Felice, and in some cases, such as in Santa Cristina, the Council of the Serene Republic ordered the return of monks and nuns to their island convents. During this period the *palude* round the island of S. Francesco increased in extent and to this day it can only be reached by boats of moderate size, and they can only move along narrow winding canals. The consequent unhealthiness and isolation forced the monks to abandon the island in about 1420. It was at this time that the island seems to have acquired the name of S. Francesco del Deserto and the brothers today still call it the Desert. The fraternity returned some thirty years later and started a period of reconstruction and adornment of the church and buildings with the assistance of rich patricians and the political backing of the doges Francesco Foscari, Pietro Mocenigo and Leonardo Loredan.

The next important crisis in the life of the island was the suppression of the monastic orders by Napoleon in 1810. The thirty-one brothers who then constituted the community were forced to leave, the island was turned into a powder magazine and the buildings used to house the garrison. Shortly afterwards Napoleon handed over the city of Venice and a large part of northern Italy to his Austrian allies. In 1856 the Emperor Francis I gave the Desert to the Patriarchate of Venice for the use in perpetuity of the Franciscan order. It took the brothers six years to restore the damage done by military occupation and they returned in 1864. The Franciscan order did not regain legal possession until the signing of the Concordat between the Church and the Italian State in 1927. Relations with the Patriarchate remained close and cordial as is shown by the continued interest in and visits to the Desert by successive Patriarchs including Pope John XXIII who was, for many years, Cardinal Patriarch of Venice.

The Concordat also cleared the way for state assistance in safeguarding the island and the conventual buildings. The Genio Civile (Public Engineering Authority) has strengthened and sometimes entirely reconstructed the island's defences against floods and tides and the Venetian

Soprintendenza ai Monumenti is in charge of the care of the church and the other ancient buildings.

The Desert continues in the even tenor of the way of St. Francis and the principles and discipline of the order he founded but this does not imply a static state. As the Father Guardian said:

'Changes have also come to S. Francesco del Deserto. As far as our discipline is concerned, one might say that we have moved from a strict, even a rigorous state of seclusion, of separation, to a more open state. Hitherto contacts with society were personal to those of our brothers whose duties, preaching or other, took them into the world. Those contacts did not affect the community, the religious family as a whole. Now it is the life of the community which has opened. The seclusion of our religious life has become less strict. For instance, visitors, pilgrim groups who come to the Desert for a day's retreat join with us religious at our meals in the refectory. Again, the rule that none but ourselves should enter the inner cloister has hitherto been meticulously observed. Now, it is possible from time to time for others to enter the cloister with the permission of the Father Superior.

One of the new activities which we are exploring here in the Desert is the provision of opportunities, for those who desire it, to share our life. To give practical effect to this innovation we are now in process of altering part of our monastic buildings to provide the necessary accommodation. Building operations have been going on for the last few months and are now nearly completed. When they are finished we shall have twenty-eight little rooms with modern plumbing and all the necessary communal rooms, with the dining-rooms served from the same kitchen as ourselves, to accommodate groups of persons, both ecclesiastic and lay, who wish to spend a few days in meditation and spiritual exercises. Besides groups we shall also take in individuals. We hope that this new activity will give rise to a new community whose aim is not seclusion but a search for a natural and appropriate extension of the lives of those of us who have chosen to live within the cloister. Those temporarily with us will be very welcome to join us in the choir,

195

in our religious exercises and in our prayers. Those who wish to work with us in our garden (hitherto restricted exclusively to the community and to the monastery servants) will be encouraged to do so because work in common is valuable in building a sense of community, of a life in common, a life of prayer, of faith, of work and discussion. This project should lead to a profitable increase in spiritual fraternal feeling. We hope that it will help to lay the ground for a more intensive contact leading to a meaningful communication, not a diffuse conversation or idle chat but communication arising from cordiality and friendliness and tending towards a constructive purpose. To attain these ends we do not restrict anyone's stay with us. You wish to come for three days? Come! But stay according to your need, to the problems besetting your spirit, to your taste; stay three days, or ten, or even a month. *Ecco!* For us the object of our welcome is that you should leave *satisfied*, with clearer ideas and a serener spirit, with a crisis surmounted or at least circumscribed and with piety re-affirmed. We have willingly undertaken this project because of our conviction of the need of the world today for a moment of spiritual stock-taking, for a moment to awaken, strengthen and enjoy a greater spiritual awareness. There are so many who are depressed and unsatisfied. The tranquillity, the peace of the Desert may help them to find more authentic values.

This was the case with a young German who came to us from Burano. He had seen our trees and our *campanile* across the lagoon and had spent half an hour in the garden talking with one of our brothers. Later that day he came back and told us how he had hoped to find in Venice an equilibrium, to heal nerves frayed by the pressures of his profession and the society in which he lived but that the noisy hotel and crowded city gave him no respite. He asked if he could stay with us for a few days. He stayed four months and left at peace and satisfied and with a clearer idea of what constitutes spiritual values. What he had been able to give him was an opportunity of making a practical experiment of the spiritual life.

We hope that the accommodation we are building will further this work, an unspectacular but fruitful work.'

The monastery buildings devoted to this new activity lie on the far side of the inner cloister and the gardens reserved for the guests face the island of S. Erasmo across the *palude*. The entrance to the buildings is by the main gardens through a gate which can be shut when there are many visitors to the island and gardens. The buildings are an L-shaped block pivoting on the monastery kitchen which will serve both the refectory of the religious family and the guests' dining-rooms. There are common rooms and libraries and accommodation for twenty-eight guests which can be sub-divided to house two groups and a number of individual visitors so arranged that each group or person can work, study, read independently. The accommodation is simple but not stark or austere.

The gardens which lie within the L of the buildings are planted with grass and flowers and young cypresses and shady trees. They continue along the embankment which stretches past the shallows separating the Desert from the neighbouring island and skirts the orchard and kitchen garden of the monastery. A new belvedere like the one facing Burano is being built on this side. When the trees and hedges have grown the gardens will have the same green peacefulness as the bird-loud main gardens. Buildings and gardens are pervaded by an atmosphere of tranquillity and human kindliness, with a care for the independence and solitude of each, mitigated for those who fear its rigours by the gentleness of the Franciscan ethos.

The Future

This portrait of the northern lagoon islands is a picture of a point in time, an attempt to catch an attitude of mind, a tone of voice at a moment of change in the life of a community and in the country of which it is a reflection.

Perhaps one of the attractions of Burano for us in our own troubled erupting industrial societies is that it is a mirror of ourselves as we were till yesterday. It is a survival of the late nineteenth century, the England of George Bourne, which is just out of reach of our memories, suddenly projected into the third quarter of the twentieth century.

Burano, so far, has only been affected by the constructive aspects of national change. Italy is a troubled country of un-disciplined, realistic, wilful people reacting against twenty years of dictatorship. She leans over backwards to be democratic and this is exploited by the sharp, the self-seeking and the dishonest, and surely everywhere there are more dishonest than honest men attracted into politics. Every-where it is easier to stop change than to make useful change and a stop may often better satisfy personal interests. Italy has not done badly in terms of men who have sought to serve her. She has done less well in terms, on the one hand, of the personal selfishness of those who cling to wealth, status, and, particularly, privilege without regard for others ('Beyond a certain social plane he never saw,' as Henry James said of the Roman prince in *The Golden Bowl*), and, on the other hand, of the grabbing tactics of those who have not had enough share in pay and regard; and each side brings out the worst in the other.

Burano has risen from penury on the national wave of prosperity of the 1960s. It has done so with a sense of wonder. It has been a like a surf-rider swept along a swell that it does not understand or want to understand. It simply wants and expects the wave to go on carrying it on. The other surf-riders know better. San Francesco del Deserto coasts along on its faith as it always has. The community of Santa Cristina has long since been overwhelmed by the breaking wave. Torcello is teetering out of balance on the curl of the wave, and knows that it will go under, that it has already lost its footing on the surfboard in the mass of water. It is only by clutching on to Burano that it can, in any sense, survive.

So what it comes to is what the future holds for Burano. What are the strengths and weaknesses with which it will face the increasing pressures of industrialisation, of a consumer society and the uncertainties of a stop and go economy?

It has been fortunate. During the years of change it has been in the eye of the storm, lying as it does on the fringe of Venice which, in spite of its own troubles, has been only remotely affected by the economic and social upheavals of Italy. It has shared the city's well-defined roots in tradition but because it has always been discounted and because of its position on the fringe, it has not, like Venice proper, been suffocated by too glorious a past and a too decrepit fabric which together have tended to stultify and embalm the minds of the Venetians. Yet it has remained firmly attached to its basic beliefs. Octavio Paz exactly described Burano's position when he wrote: *'Une société est constitúee par ses institutions, ses créations intellectuelles et artistiques, ses techniques, sa vie matérielle et spirituelle. Elle est aussi ce qui se trouve derrière et au-dessous de tout cela'*, and goes on to refer to what Ortega y Gasset called the marrow of history. The marrow of Burano is the extraordinary strength and resistance of the community. This has enabled it to move leisurely, and perhaps with too much self-confidence, to a position from which it can advance into the future while re- taining the solidity of its tradition. This is in notable contrast to the social disarray of the uprooted working populations of Southern Italy set down to rebuild their lives without much help in the industrial centres of the North.

Paradoxically enough one of the strengths on which Burano has been able to count has been its geographical situation which has both isolated it and confined it to a small island. The Buranello is passionately chauvinistic, his *campanile storto* (crooked church tower) constantly recurs in his conversation and is a comfort to him even on the horizon. He does not move away unless he is forced to and returns as soon as he can. He loves this warm close womb which shel- ters him. He loves and maintains the way he and his fathers have always lived while enjoying every minute of his new- found, and very relative, affluence. The cohesion of his com- munity owes much to the fact that it cannot expand. Burano is a small, crowded, built-up island. There can be no question of finding more room by building high because of the unstable lagoon bottom. So Burano must always be limited in size and can never be subjected to large-scale mun- icipal housing or unplanned speculative building. It can never be a Mestre, a soulless, formless jungle. The restriction of Burano is natural, a fact of geography. By contrast the growth of Torcello is restricted artificially since it is scheduled as a national monument. Given its marvellous monuments and atmosphere one would not wish it other- wise, but one should, nevertheless, recognise that putting a dead stop to development without providing a livelihood for the rural population has killed a community.

Burano's pride in being different from other people is also important in its survival as a community. This is a common

*Octavio Paz — Introduction to *Quetzalcóatl et Guadalupe* by Jacques Lafaye.

feeling in Venice and prevailed, they say, between one *sestriere* and another though the differences in dialect and attitude now seem to have been whittled down to friendly abuse. Burano's feeling of being different nearly always carries the implication that the others simply do not know what they are doing. One cannot but notice for instance the tone of contempt in which one is told, 'Here we eat little artichokes. On the *terraferma* they eat them when they are much bigger.'

Burano wears its own tradition and singularity proudly but lightly as a customary, everyday thing. They all feel the same. As they say, 'There are no *signori* in Burano.' There is a strength as well as a feeling of protection for individuals in being a one-class society. It cannot be torn apart by social divisions and, being fairly indifferent to politics, it is not given to that sort of dissension.

Within this placid, close-knit society there is an interlocking network of family loyalties, connections and alliances. This makes for a helpful, kind society. It is not much given to moral judgments and is, on the whole, tolerant of the vagaries of others, but it can be cruel to those who overstep the limits of the permitted. It is a provident society and regards the considerable sums now spent on house renovations, furniture, kitchen equipment, boats and outboard motors as investments. The Buranello version of Veblen's conspicuous waste', which includes lavish gifts, gorgeous weddings and a better whatever-it-is than the neighbours have is not only condoned, but required by the community. They have, nevertheless, remained a frugal people, in spite of their newly-acquired taste for meat. They all remember poverty and know that improvidence is dangerous. And they are right. Even in these times when social services are available the Italian bureaucratic machine is so old-fashioned, unwieldy and dilatory that it can take months for old-age and disability pensions, maternity and children's allowances to come through.

The weaknesses in Burano are chiefly that it is too confident, too self-sufficient and too self-satisfied. It is an intensely self-regardant society, as are perhaps all confident, settled societies. It is not interested in other people's attitudes

201

or thoughts or cultures. It is not looking for anything new. It is quite sure that it has found all that it needs or wants. This in the long run will breed spots of softness which will decay the vigour which the community derived from having to fight to survive. Its self-satisfaction is already creating an immobility which offends the intelligent young. They already find Burano claustrophobic. What most members of any society, particularly the young and rebellious, notice about it are its disadvantages, its restrictive and repressive aspects, its taboos. In Burano, the intelligent young, who see careers ahead and the possibility of moving into the while-collar and professional categories, are not frightened of the outside world. As the first generation of a financially viable community they do not feel the need to retreat from a hostile world (usually felt to be Venice) to the warm, affectionate, known situation in their own island. They have a deep feeling for the community but they are not blind to its shortcomings. They know that, for themselves, the balance of advantage lies in mixing with the world. They want to take Burano along with them in change and renovation to suit their own kind of people and expectations. Burano has reached a plateau, perhaps even a doldrum in its evolution. If these young people are not allowed, by the inertia of the mass, to make changes and to modernise, they will go. If they go Burano will be left without leaders and the community will be diminished.

Burano must look to its own resources and cure it own weaknesses to avoid this decay. It has the resilience and tenacity to find a way to preserve its traditions adapted to the world of tomorrow. It cannot depend on anyone else.

Willy Brandt once said of Berlin: 'Here one is not faced with problems of high policy; one deals with living people whom one can help.'* This is what the national government, the authorities of the regions, the provinces, the municipalities of Italy, the possessing social classes have not yet maybe cannot recognise. Italy needs a Willy Brandt. But then, which of us does not?

*Quoted by Terence Prittie in *Willy Brandt: Portrait of a Statesman.*

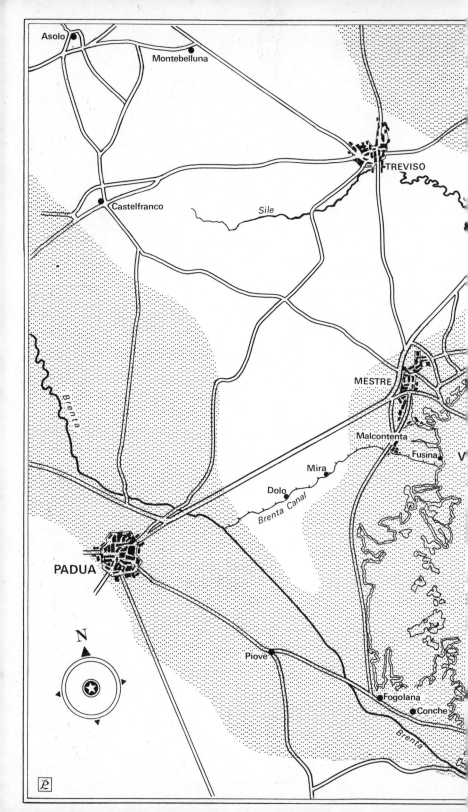